MOSES

For Marilyn,
Many blessings! Hope
you enjoy this exploration
of Moses through
contemporary eyes!
                    Blessings,
            Rabbi Maurice Harris

MOSES

A Stranger among Us

Maurice D. Harris

with a Foreword by Rev. Daniel Bryant

CASCADE *Books* · Eugene, Oregon

MOSES
A Stranger among Us

Cascade Books
A Division of Wipf and Stock Publishers
199 W. 8th Ave., Suite 3
Eugene, OR 97401

www.wipfandstock.com

ISBN 13: 978-1-61097-407-3

Cataloging-in-Publication data:

Harris, Maurice D.

Moses : a stranger among us / Maurice D. Harris.

xxvi + 138 p. ; 23 cm. Includes bibliographical references.

ISBN 13: 978-1-61097-407-3

1. Moses (Biblical leader). 2 . Bible. O.T. Pentateuch—Criticism, interpretations, etc. 3.Abrahamic religions. I. Title.

BS580.M6 H44 2012

Manufactured in the U.S.A.

For my parents,
William I. Harris, of blessed memory,
and Marie Harris

Contents

Foreword

MOSES IS EASY TO spot in ancient iconography. He is almost always portrayed as holding a scroll representing the Torah or tablets of stone representing the Ten Commandments. In more recent art Moses may be shown with the burning bush or splitting the Red Sea, but still easy to recognize. From Michelangelo to Cecil B. DeMille, Moses has been universally portrayed in art and film as a towering figure with flowing beard who commands obedience even from forces of nature. Those iconic images represent the popular Moses, the familiar figure known to not only Jews and Christians, but people of all and no faith traditions.

We all recognize Moses because we think we know him, or at least we know about him. But would we know the man surrounded by five determined sisters who think they can challenge the law given by God? Or how often have we considered the possibility that the marriage of Moses to Tzipporah is a model of interfaith marriage? Would we recognize a Moses who, instead of "laying down the law" for all to follow and obey, shows adaptability and willingness to incorporate ideas and principles from other cultures?

In the pages that follow Rabbi Maurice Harris presents us with "the Moses we never knew," or to borrow a title from Marcus Borg writing about the historical Jesus, here you will be "meeting Moses again for the first time." This is not, however, an attempt to give us the "historical Moses" apart from the biblical story. As Harris notes in chapter 10, the nature of the sources, the scarcity of other historical and archaeological evidence, and just the historical distance between us and Moses make it virtually impossible to engage in the same kind of historical analysis that has been done around the person of Jesus of Nazareth. For Harris as well as for most followers of the Abrahamic traditions, be they Jew, Christian, or Muslim, what really matters is not the historical person *behind* the tradition, but "the person found in the Jewish sacred literature." This is the Moses who has grown to be such an influential figure in the biblical tradition and who, for those who are willing to engage him as does Harris, challenges us, inspires us, and still can lead us through wildernesses and to mountaintops on our own spiritual journeys today.

It would be a mistake, however, to view this book simply as a fresh look at a familiar face, as needed as that may be in the case of Moses. Harris does much more than give us new insights into this gigantic figure of the biblical story. In telling the stories of Moses largely ignored in popular portrayals (including those given from the pulpit), Harris gives us new insight into faith itself. His view on the nature of "followers" vs. "participants" (chapter 8) is a gem for all religious traditions. As we say in the pulpit profession, "That will preach!" We are all familiar with the importance of law in the Torah. In chapter 7 Harris shows us the importance of *story* and how story and law have a reciprocal relationship guided by the claims of justice. That too will preach.

This is not to suggest that preachers will benefit most from this book. Far from it. Anyone who considers Moses to be an important figure in their tradition or in the history of civilization will find something here, like the proverbial manna in the wilderness, to chew on. And when fully digested, the nourishment they gain will benefit the soul, just as we learn from the tradition of Moses, "that one does not live by bread alone, but by every word that comes from the mouth of the LORD."[1] And as Harris makes evident, that word did not cease coming to be with the death of Moses, the completion of the Torah, the compilation of the Hebrew Scriptures nor the addition of all other Jewish, Christian, or Islamic texts, but has continued to evolve and speaks to us in our modern world today.

Daniel E. H. Bryant
Senior Minister
First Christian Church (Disciples of Christ)
Eugene, OR

1. Deut 8:3b, *NRSV*.

Acknowledgments

MANY PEOPLE HELPED MAKE this book possible, and I am deeply grateful to all of them. First and foremost I want to thank my wife, Melissa Crabbe, who provided moral support, editorial suggestions, inspiration, and ideas.

Several mentors and colleagues from the seminary I attended, the Reconstructionist Rabbinical College (RRC), offered editorial feedback that was extremely helpful. I want to thank Rabbis Nancy Fuchs-Kramer and David Teutsch for taking the time to read through the manuscript and offer editorial suggestions and advice about seeking publication. Dr. Elsie Stern of RRC helped me with questions I had about academic biblical scholarship. I would feel remiss if I didn't say that Dr. S. Tamar Kamionkowski, my Bible professor at RRC, encouraged me several years ago to write about the Bible even though I don't have a doctorate in the subject. I'm grateful to her for that encouragement, and for being the teacher who opened my eyes to the amazing world of the Hebrew Bible. I also want to thank all my teachers at RRC, an institution that has so profoundly shaped my values and my approach to Judaism.

I'm grateful to Rabbi Carol Caine, a friend and colleague, who offered very helpful editorial suggestions. Thank you to Rabbis Michael Fessler, Nancy Fuchs-Kramer, Jason Klein, Sue Levy, and Goldie Milgram for responding to a question I posed to rabbinic colleagues online about the uses of trope to offer comment on parts of the Torah that present problematic or troubling content.

Thanks to Ellen Frankel, Pamela Tamarkin Reis, and Lawrence Bush for taking the time to read some of the early material and for offering advice about publishing. I also want to thank people in the Eugene, Oregon area who were generous with their time and their willingness to offer me very helpful feedback on the manuscript. Dr. Steven Shankman of the University of Oregon Humanities Center and Classics Department of-fered editorial feedback, and Dr. Deborah Green of the Harold Schnitzer Family Program in Judaic Studies at the University of Oregon offered as-sistance as well. My friend and fellow writer Barry Nobel gave me detailed feedback on the manuscript. Ellen Todras and Gary Tepfer provided great feedback and encouragement. Thank you also to Vic Hansen, whose ob-servation in one of the adult education classes I taught at Temple Beth Israel in Eugene proved helpful in one of the chapters.

In the local Christian community, I want to thank my good friends Rev. Dan Bryant, Rev. Melanie Oommen, and Gay Kramer-Dodd for giv-ing me feedback on the manuscript and on its potential for being mean-ingful to Christians as well as Jews. I am also indebted to Rev. Dan Bryant for writing the Foreword to this book.

I want to thank Dr. Jacob L. Wright, Assistant Professor of Hebrew Bible at Emory University's Candler School of Theology, for reading the manuscript, offering suggestions about my research into Numbers 31, and encouraging me to keep working on the book.

I owe a debt to the instructors I learned from at the Summer Peacebuilding Institute of Eastern Mennonite University in Harrisonburg, Virginia. Dr. Ron Kraybill and Dr. Robert Eisen, two of the instructors I had in the course I took in 2006, "Religion: Source of Conflict, Resource for Peace," especially helped me develop some of the core values I share in this book.

I want to thank my friend Ted Lewis for making an introduction for me to Wipf & Stock Publishers. I'm also appreciative of Christian Amondson's time and efforts at Wipf & Stock, and of the contributions made by Dr. Robin Parry, my editor at Wipf & Stock.

I couldn't have written this book if I hadn't spent the past eight years as a congregational rabbi at Temple Beth Israel in Eugene, Oregon. The congregation gave me the opportunity to write and deliver many sermons, and it was that experience—along with the positive feedback and encour-agement I received from members of the congregation—that enabled me to conceive of this book. I want to thank the entire community of Temple Beth Israel for being the warm, diverse, engaging, and open-minded con-gregation that it is.

I'm deeply grateful to my mentor and colleague of these past eight years, Rabbi Yitzhak Husbands-Hankin, the Senior Rabbi at Temple Beth Israel. His ethical example and serious yet open-minded engagement with Jewish texts and tradition have been an inspiration for me, and have influenced my approach to the subjects treated in this book. I also thank Yedida Bessemer for her willingness to absorb some of my duties in the Talmud Torah religious school while I was taking time off to work on this book, and for her constant encouragement. Thanks as well to Nina Korican, Shirley Shiffman, Randy Perkal and Jacque Albert in the office at Temple Beth Israel for your support and friendship during my transition towards a career path more focused on writing and teaching.

I want to thank my mom, Marie Harris, for her lifetime of encouragement, and especially for her support for my writing. I also give thanks to my father of blessed memory, William Harris, for being a mentor and teacher whose sensitivity to others' feelings and ethics have guided me in every way. Heartfelt thanks to Bob and Glenda Crabbe for their unwavering support and love, and to Robert Crabbe for his generosity, including the gift of the computer I used to write this book. I can't say enough to thank my wife, Melissa Crabbe, and my children, Clarice and Hunter, for their constant love and support.

Finally, I offer thanks to the Source of Life for the joy and satisfaction of reaching the milestone of having my first book published. I hope that this book serves a good purpose and contributes positively in some small way to others.

Abbreviations

BT   Babylonian Talmud

FOX   Everett Fox, *The Five Books of Moses: The Schocken Bible,
            Volume 1, A New English Translation with Commentary
            and Notes*. New York: Schocken, 1995.

m.   Mishnah

NIV   New International Version

NRSV   New Revised Standard Version

OJPS   Jewish Publication Society 1917 Translation

Shakir   Online Quran Project—M. H. Shakir translation.
            Online: http://www.al-quran.info

Introduction

THIS IS A BOOK about the Moses we don't usually hear about—not in religious school or from the pulpit. And that's a shame, because more people would relate to Moses and find him a compelling figure if, more often, our religious teachers would go beyond the familiar caricatures of him. By shining light on aspects of his story and character that are rarely discussed, we meet the Moses who speaks to a wide range of people's circumstances today. We get to bring Moses down from his exalted pedestal, where he was never very comfortable anyway. We meet Moses the adopted child; Moses the ex-con; Moses the failure; Moses the intermarrier.

And by turning the spotlight on several of the often overlooked people whose courage and cleverness made his extraordinary life possible, we get to see how much his greatest achievements depended upon others. Rather than being the result of God working mainly through one man's bold actions, the exodus from Egypt and the transformation of the Hebrews from slaves to a free nation took place because of many individuals' brave and creative resistance to an immense, oppressive power structure. We get to see the divinely inspired women and men—Israelites and non-Israelites—who made Moses' leadership possible.

Finally, by stepping outside the limits of traditional religious interpretations of biblical texts, we get to see Moses in fresh, new ways that teach us about our values as well as those of our ancestors. Modern academic biblical scholarship lets us study the historical development of the literary character of Moses and glimpse the workings of "mythopeosis, 'the making of myth,' [the] means by which [humankind] discerns and conveys truths otherwise inexpressible."[1] Each of the ten chapters that fol-

1. Levenson, *Sinai and Zion,* 104–5.

lows focuses on one aspect of Moses that is either generally overlooked or not thought of at all in mainstream religious presentations of Moses. My hope is that the Moses who may be unfamiliar to us is a figure who can renew our interest in essential spiritual and ethical questions facing humanity today.

I wrote this book for a general audience who already know the basic story of Moses' life as presented in the Hebrew Bible (or Old Testament, for Christians), even if that familiarity comes mainly from a hazily remembered past of Sunday school sessions and Charlton Heston. If you know what the golden calf, the ten plagues, and manna are, for example, but you don't know the name of the place where Moses struck the rock instead of speaking to it as God had directed him, then you know enough to follow me in this book. If you have a significantly deeper knowledge of Moses, either from religiously or academically oriented study, please bear with me when I occasionally provide more explanation than you require. Even those of you who know a lot about Moses will, I hope, still benefit from this book.

Also, I want to mention that in many ways this is a Jewish book—the product of a rabbi interested in issues that directly face the contemporary Jewish community. And yet, I am confident that readers of other religions or no religion can also find much of value here.

If I had to categorize this book, I would call it a homiletical book. For people not familiar with the terminology of clergy, homiletical writing is sermonic. In my sermons I often take several biblical and rabbinic texts and explore them, but I stop short of going into too much detail about textual particulars because it's easy to lose one's audience in too much minutiae and because the purpose of a sermon is ultimately to inspire. In sermons I also explore biblical texts by using multiple ways of reading and interpreting them, often freely switching from one method of interpretation to another. So for instance, I might begin by examining the importance of a linguistic feature of a word in biblical Hebrew, then shift to citing early rabbinic midrash[2] on the passage, and conclude by drawing upon insights developed by academic biblical scholarship. I offer my sermons as my personal responses to the Bible, not as the "correct" response.

---

2. Midrash refers to the set of methods that the ancient rabbis used to interpret and expand upon the texts of the Hebrew Bible. More will be said about the nature of midrash later.

My goal is to engage in a contemporary dialogue of meaning with the biblical text, and only secondarily to make a contribution to religious or academic biblical scholarship. The result is an eclectic approach to reading the Bible, and that's what I offer in this book. I've spent considerable time with the Torah's texts about Moses, and I've discovered certain ways of looking at the texts that have sparked questions and ideas within me about life, truth, and higher meaning.

Like many before me, in taking the time to pay close attention to the biblical accounts of Moses, I've discovered Moses to be a surprisingly complicated and compelling figure who shouldn't be reduced to a cartoon character shouting, "Let my people go!" or a stern old man coming down from the mountain carrying stone tablets of the Law. As the philosopher Sam Keen wrote, "Sooner or later something occurs in all cultures and individuals to smash the accepted answers and leave agonizing questions in its place . . . The spiritual quest begins when we turn away from our standard answers and turn toward fresh questions."[3] Keen could have been writing about Moses with these words. Moses' story is a story of an individual and an entire people embarking on just this kind of spiritual quest, leaving behind the gods and folkways of the mightiest and most influential empire on earth, and venturing out into the wilderness—the unknown—in search of a new way to be. In our contemporary society, with its tendency towards clichéd portraits of religious giants, it turns out that the Moses who led this battered people out of slavery is someone we may hardly know at all. He is truly a stranger among us.

***

And now, here is a brief preview of each of the ten chapters of this book:

In the Jewish world, Moses is usually described as the consummate *insider* of our tradition because of his close relationship with God and his role in communicating the divine commandments to the Israelites. But the Torah goes to great lengths to show us in Moses a man who actually lived most of his life as an *outsider* to the Israelites. Chapter 1 of this book, "Moses the Outsider," takes a look at Moses from this perspective. His upbringing in the Pharaoh's court, his marriage to a non-Israelite woman, and even his failure to set foot in the sacred land of his people all place

3. Keen, *Hymns to an Unknown God*, 14.

him at the margins of the Israelite community. Moses is, in fact, both an outsider and an insider—something that makes him surprisingly relevant to the many Jews and Christians today who find themselves simultaneously drawn to and uncomfortable with their faith traditions.

In chapter 2, "The Women Who Saved Moses: Civil Disobedience and the Seeds of Redemption," our focus turns from Moses himself to five women in his early life who chose not to cooperate with the Pharaoh's laws. Their acts of civil disobedience drive the drama of the beginning of the book of Exodus, and their resistance makes Moses' life possible (and, therefore, the grand stories of Judaism and Christianity alike). Like many of the underexamined aspects of the story of Moses that this book discusses, the role of these women's subversive and ethical resistance to a system of oppression is prominently featured in the Torah. It is not the Torah text that has covered over their actions, but rather our own tendencies to highlight other aspects of Moses' story and minimize the importance of these women.

Chapter 3, "Mother of Moses, Princess of Egypt," focuses on one of the five brave women discussed in chapter 2. Zooming in on those first few seconds when the Pharaoh's daughter looked at the baby she found floating in a basket upon the Nile, this chapter examines the moment when her heart filled with compassion, leading her to choose to save the Hebrew baby's life despite her father's decree. This instant flash of compassion changed history. The deliberate attention the Torah gives this crucial moment invites us to scrutinize this episode in baby Moses' life, and yet it is usually presented as a prelude to the "real action" of the Moses story. How unfortunate, because in this single moment the Torah offers us the opportunity to study the nature of the inherent instability of even the most powerful and entrenched systems of oppression. No empire, no totalitarian system can stop the unpredictable emergence of compassion in the human heart. Chapter 3 examines how the story of Moses' rescue on the waters of the Nile teaches us about the resiliency and unpredictability of the human urge towards love, meaning, and truth.

Moving forward in Moses' life, chapter 4, "Moses and Tzipporah: When Intermarriage Is Good for the Jews," examines the way that Moses' marriage to a Midianite woman, Tzipporah, is positively presented in the Torah. This chapter (more than any other in the book) addresses an issue of great immediate concern within the contemporary Jewish community.

Over the last decades, American Jewish leaders have been having an anxious and emotionally charged internal conversation on the implications of widespread Jewish intermarriage in the United States. Rabbis and other Jewish leaders have been vigorously debating what the healthiest Jewish communal responses to intermarriage are.

Of course, many non-Jewish religious and ethnic groups also are facing anxiety and uncertainty over rapidly changing societal norms around intermarriage, and this aspect of Moses' life provides insight into the cross-cultural and interreligious boundary questions that intermarriage inevitably raises. This chapter investigates the way that the Hebrew Bible presents multiple portraits of intermarriage. In some cases, it depicts intermarriage as a dangerous and corrupting influence, while in other cases it describes these relationships positively and displays the ways in which Israelite life was strengthened because of intermarriage. Such is the case with Moses, whose Midianite wife and father-in-law make essential contributions to Moses' and the Israelites' survival and development.

Chapter 5, "Moses and Jethro: Religion as a Creative Open System," takes one episode in the story of Moses discussed in chapter 4 and uses it as a jumping off point for examining an important aspect of Moses' leadership style. The episode is the one in which Moses' father-in-law, Jethro, visits Moses shortly after he and the Israelites have successfully left Egypt and are encamped in the wilderness. Jethro sees Moses operating as the only judge and arbiter of disputes among the entire Israelite nation, and he warns Moses that this is a recipe for burnout and failure. Jethro urges Moses to delegate authority to a multilevel system of judges and courts, and Moses readily accepts the advice.

Jethro is a Midianite priest, a non-Israelite who loves and cares for Moses and his people. This chapter examines how Moses' receptivity to Jethro's ideas illustrates Moses' willingness to treat his religion as a "creative open system." "Creative open system" is a term used by scientists who study chaos and complexity theory, and such systems are found in natural phenomena as well as in human organizations. Moses is rarely presented to us as the kind of leader who encouraged his people to pay close attention to the ideas, beliefs, and methods of other peoples. On the contrary, far more often we hear about his condemnations of other nations' practices and beliefs. The reality is that the Torah presents us with both images of Moses, and this chapter seeks to cast some badly needed light on the ways that Moses and later Jewish tradition time and time again have operated on a basis of creative openness to the outside world.

Chapter 6 is called "Moses and God: *Panim-El-Panim, Ehyeh-Asher-Ehyeh*." The Hebrew in the chapter's title is taken from two key phrases that the Torah presents during Moses' encounters with God. *Panim-El-Panim* means "face to face," which is the language the Torah more than once uses to describe how Moses and God interact. *Ehyeh-Asher-Ehyeh* means "I will be what I will be," or "I am that I am," and these are the cryptic words that God uses to answer Moses when Moses asks to know God's name. This chapter examines the different ways that the human-Divine relationship is portrayed in the Torah in the interactions between Moses and God. Moses is paradoxically presented to us as a man who spoke with God face to face, and yet who was also told by God that no human could see God's face and live. Treating the Torah as a text that intends us to wrestle with this seeming contradiction, we explore the question of how or when we encounter God in our lives.

In chapter 7, "The Law of Moses Can Be Challenged and Changed," our attention turns to one of the Torah's most vivid descriptions of the actual workings of the Israelites' legal system. We get to see the Law of Moses in action. Of course, the Law of Moses is, according to Jewish tradition, the Law of God. Before the rise of the modern liberal movements (denominations) of Judaism, rabbis universally taught that the Torah's divine laws are immutable and perfect.[4] But does the Torah text itself truly advocate the idea that the Law of Moses is immutable and perfect? This chapter examines two episodes in the Torah in which a group of average Israelites bring an appeal to Moses for particular laws to be reconsidered. Each group makes an argument that following the law as it is will result in an injustice. Moses' leadership style in these scenes is to listen carefully and then take the appeal directly to God. In each instance, God then approves legal changes in response to the appeals.

---

4. Judaism's sacred literature of legal interpretation, the Talmud, has used interpretive tools to bring about many changes to the Torah's laws. The traditional Jewish belief in the perfection and immutability of the Torah's laws has functioned within a religious system that had mechanisms for legal change. The sages would usually bring about these legal changes, however, without asserting that the Torah's laws had *actually* been changed, but rather that proper rabbinic interpretation had revealed the correct way of understanding what the Torah "actually meant."

Chapter 8 is called "The Voice of Pain and Cruelty in Moses." When rabbis and Christian ministers seek to engage their congregants in discussions about what we can learn from Moses, they rarely ask them to consider whether we might feel morally compelled to disagree with some of the things in the Torah that Moses does at God's command. Though religious traditionalists might see this as a heretical idea, I believe that by taking an attitude of truly open inquiry towards sacred texts, we can sometimes learn and grow by asking questions that religious dogma might forbid. One such question is, can we sometimes learn moral truth from the way the Torah presents Moses and God by identifying ways in which we do *not* want to be like them?

Chapter 8 begins this inquiry by focusing on Numbers 31, in which God instructs Moses to order the Israelites to commit genocide against another people. I use this disturbing episode in the Torah as a launching point for a rigorous discussion of the dangers of dogmatically following any sacred text or religious leader. The chapter concludes by offering ideas about how religious communities today can identify dangerous sacred texts and work with them in creative new ways that disarm their potential for encouraging violence, cruelty, and false ideas about God.

Chapter 9 is called "*Rav Lach*: Moses Experiences Life's Harsh Boundaries." The Hebrew words *rav lach* are idiomatic. The literal translation is something like "this is enough for you." Figuratively, *rav lach* means, "Whoa, you're asking for too much!" or, "What you've already gotten is all that you should get—it's not your place to ask for anything more." "*Rav lach*" is the way God says no to Moses when Moses appeals to God for the final time to be allowed to enter the Promised Land. Rather than pursuing the commonly asked question of why God prohibited Moses from entering the Land of Israel even but once, this chapter instead explores what our options for coping are as people who are sometimes forced by the human condition to live with life's harsh pronouncements. Chapter 9 also investigates the flip side of our greatest disappointments: life's unexpected opportunities for higher meaning and joy.

Chapter 10 is called "'Moses'" with intentional quotation marks. During the last two centuries, academic biblical scholarship has advanced the theory that the Torah was edited together out of several major source materials, and that the final version was completed roughly twenty-five hundred years ago. According to this theory, the literary character of

Moses that we encounter in the Bible is a composite figure, one made up of materials from several different sources. Many of these materials were written centuries after Moses' life, and therefore include the distorting influences of legend, polemics, and the human imagination. Hence, it might be appropriate to talk sometimes about "Moses," the composite character made up of many different elements, as opposed to the historical Moses of flesh and blood.

Because this approach to Torah is contrary to the traditional religious doctrine of the Torah's having been authored by God, we generally don't hear Moses discussed in these terms. And yet the shame of this is that there is so much that we can learn by taking the time to look at the constructed nature of the character of "Moses."

Chapter 10 starts by drawing inspiration from work that has been going on for over twenty years among a group of Christian Bible scholars who have been endeavoring to try to distinguish between those sayings attributed to Jesus in the New Testament that are most likely to be authentic to the historical Jesus, versus those sayings most likely to have been developed by later groups of his followers and attributed to him. These Bible scholars make a distinction between the historical Jesus and the "Jesus" presented in the New Testament, whom they understand to be a composite literary figure.

After briefly examining some of the possible literary strands that, woven together, make up the "Moses" of the Torah, the chapter turns to the way that "Moses" has been repeatedly reimagined and reconstructed over the centuries by later generations of Jews. Then, the chapter looks at how "Moses" has also been reworked in Christian and Muslim sacred texts and traditions.

***

Finally, a word about me and my background. I was trained as a rabbi at the Reconstructionist Rabbinical College in Philadelphia, and following my ordination in 2003 I served a synagogue in Eugene, Oregon, for eight years. As a lover of Jewish texts and a spiritual seeker, I found my place in the world of committed Jewish life within Reconstructionism. This particular approach to Judaism—and to religion in general—so deeply influences me that its imprint is all over this book. A few words about "where I'm coming from" as a Reconstructionist, therefore, would be useful.

Reconstructionism regards Judaism as an evolving religious civilization and celebrates Judaism as a living, dynamic system. This is an approach to Judaism that takes tradition seriously while also maintaining an openness to creative, constructive change. Its philosophy is one that is committed to total freedom of inquiry and intellectual honesty, while simultaneously engaging Jewish sacred texts and traditions with depth, vibrancy, and moral and spiritual seeking. Reconstructionism encourages the members of local Jewish communities to take the time to study Jewish sacred texts and the evolution of Jewish thought and practice, and then to arrive at contemporary forms of Jewish belief and ritual that reflect a synthesis of what tradition has to teach combined with our own lived experiences of truth.

If you were to visit a Reconstructionist synagogue for Sabbath services, most likely what you would encounter would be a warm and down-to-earth prayer service led in part by laypeople, and marked by much Hebrew singing and chanting as well as group discussion of a section of the Torah. It would have a more traditional feel and aesthetic than most services in Reform synagogues, but somewhat less traditional than typical Conservative services.

If you were familiar with the traditional Hebrew liturgy, then at a Reconstructionist service you would also notice some creative liturgical changes designed to express values such as gender equality, the full acceptance and affirmation of gays and lesbians, and the rejection of any notion that Judaism or Jews are more special to God than other religious traditions or peoples. The aim of this kind of prayer service is a serious engagement with tradition merged with a willingness to make thoughtful changes that reflect emerging understandings of truth that may contradict earlier traditional beliefs.

For readers who may be more familiar with Christian theological terminology, Reconstructionist Judaism does not believe in the idea of what some Christian theologians call *biblical inerrancy*. Our approach to the Torah is one that combines reverence for the text with an understanding that the Torah was written by our ancestors, who wove multiple source materials together over time to form the final document. We have awe for the Torah's infinite depths and endless capacity for inspiration and moral teaching, in keeping with the Talmudic passage that poses the question: "'Why were the words of Torah compared to a fig tree?' The sages replied: 'Because figs don't all ripen at the same time, the more one searches among the branches of the tree, the more figs one finds in it. Similarly, with the words of Torah, the more we study them, the more illuminating insights we find.'"[5]

And yet, a Reconstructionist approach to the Torah (and all our sacred texts) also acknowledges that, like all things crafted by human beings, they are flawed texts that at times we may not agree with morally or spiritually. We are intimately *engaged* with our sacred texts, but not ultimately *commanded* by them. To borrow the words of the contemporary Christian theologian Marcus J. Borg, we take the Bible seriously, but not literally.[6] A famous motto of the Reconstructionist movement is "the past has a vote, not a veto." In the pages that follow, my training and philosophy will be apparent.

***

A note about terminology and this book: I sometimes use the words "Jew" and "Israelite," as well as variants of both words, interchangeably in my discussions, even though an historian would call biblical characters "Hebrews" or "Israelites," and wait until the Second Temple period, beginning about 2,500 years ago, before employing the term "Jew." The term "Jew" refers to the Israelites who lived in the territory of Judah (one of the original twelve Israelite tribes), and it didn't become the primary name for the entire people of Israel until Second Temple times.

So why am I imprecise with these terms? For a few reasons. Sometimes the method I'm using to examine a biblical text is grounded in traditional Jewish interpretations like midrash, and the rabbis tended to be historically anachronistic. For example, they call Moses "Moses-our-rabbi" even though Moses had never heard of a rabbi. Similarly, the rabbinic tradition thinks of Abraham, Sarah, and their biblical descendants as the first Jews,

5. This is a paraphrasing of the Babylonian Talmud, BT Eruvin 54b, along with Rashi's comment on the passage.

6. Borg, *Reading the Bible Again for the First Time: Taking the Bible Seriously but Not Literally.* I'm referencing part of the title of this book.

because the rabbis saw themselves and their religious practices as being in continuity with those of their biblical ancestors.

Another reason I sometimes conflate "Israelite" and "Jew" is that this is one of the poetic licenses that rabbis often take in sermons. In the Jewish community, we identify tribally and spiritually with the Torah's stories and characters, and so we often freely talk about Moses leading the *Jews* to freedom out of Egypt, not the "Hebrews" or "Israelites." For example, during the holiday of Passover, we in the Jewish community talk of the story of the exodus from Egypt as happening to *us*, not only to our ancestors. In doing so, we express a spiritual connection, not an historical description, when we use the term "Jews" to describe Israelites. I ask you to indulge my occasional collapsing of these terms as you encounter them. With that in mind, it is time to meet Moses again, perhaps for the first time.

1

Moses the Outsider

"I was a stranger in a strange land."
—Moses[1]

JONATHAN KIRSCH, THE AUTHOR of *Moses: A Life,* wrote, "The real Moses—the Moses no one knows—was someone far richer and stranger than we are customarily allowed to see."[2] On Yom Kippur[3] 2007, I gave a sermon to my congregation in which I hoped to illustrate Kirsch's point. Here's how I began:

> There's a member of the Jewish community who I'd like to talk about this evening—someone who has lived an extraordinary life. I haven't told him beforehand that he would be the focus of my talk, so I don't know how he might react. He's someone who has lived a life that is so compelling, so filled with controversy and contradiction, that on this sacred day when we make time to re-

1. Exod 2:22
2. Kirsch, *Moses: A Life,* 2.
3. Yom Kippur is the Day of Atonement, the holiest day of the year in Judaism. Jews fast for an entire day, from one sundown to the next, and gather at the synagogue for lengthy prayer services. The theme of the day is seeking forgiveness and renewing one's intentions to live a more moral and spiritually attuned life. The first religious service of the holy day is called Kol Nidrey and it takes place at sundown on the 10th day of the Hebrew month of Tishrei. Many Jews who rarely go to synagogue come to Kol Nidrey, and it is common for a rabbi to give a major sermon during this service.

flect on the meaning of our lives, I was drawn to talk about what his life might mean to all of us.

His is not the classic "nice Jewish boy makes good" story. Let me start at the beginning. He was born Jewish, but persecution and chaotic political times left him orphaned and adopted by a non-Jewish family. They were prominent, well-to-do people with clout and social status.

As a young child he was told about his Jewish background, and he struggled with complex identity issues throughout his youth. He was, of course, accustomed to the family he'd grown up with, but he was also alienated from them and their elite friends, particularly their ostentatious wealth and insensitivity to social injustice.

He became pretty mixed up as a young man and had problems with his temper, at times becoming violent. Eventually he got into serious trouble with the law. He killed a man—he says it was an accident; a witness said it wasn't. He fled the jurisdiction and then the country, and he was convicted in court *in absentia*. Now an ex-con and a fugitive, his life was in a shambles. His adoptive parents became confused and devastated. For his own protection, he laid low in the rural margins of his new country.

I think one of the reasons I'm so interested in this person's life is that his story completely defies the stereotypes we tend to associate with Jewish men, and yet despite that he would go on to contribute so much to Jewish life. Jewish men, they say, are smart, sensitive, educated, gentle, stable, and good providers. As my wife, Melissa's, Auntie Kim, who is Chinese, said to her approvingly after meeting me and sizing me up—"Good match! Steady boy, not playboy. Good match." Auntie Kim would not have approved of the man I'm talking about tonight: an orphaned ex-con fugitive with no money, legal problems a mile long, and anger management issues.

There's another important piece to his story—one that he didn't like talking about. He had a disability that was embarrassing to him, and being mocked for it early in life may have accounted for his temper. It was a speech disorder that got worse the more anxious he became, a kind of stutter and getting stuck verbally under stress. It got in the way of a lot of things. It embarrassed his refined, high-born parents. His disability also seemed unmanly in the macho culture he grew up in. And it made him stand out, which was something he never liked. This was a man who didn't seek attention at all, and being noticed was especially difficult for him.

Anyway, after some years passed, the legal case against him back home went cold. His adoptive parents grew old and never got over their loss, and he didn't keep in touch with them. In his new country he found modest work as an undocumented immigrant and basically kept to himself. The Jewish demographers who publish anxious reports about intermarriage would not be thrilled that he intermarried—twice, actually, over the course of his life. Many rabbis might chafe over the fact that he never set foot once in a synagogue or belonged to a single Jewish organization—not even a Jewish Community Center. The Federation folks might gossip that he never wrote a single check to a Jewish charity.[4]

With this kind of background, he went on to do a number of things that have had a profound influence on Jewish life and on radical politics, too, including the contemporary Liberation Theology movement and other causes ranging from anti-sweatshop campaigns to anti-poverty activism. The turning point in his life came in his older age, when he decided, for the first time, to act definitively on his Jewish identity and get involved in the needs of the Jewish community. He was a man with rough edges who became an important Jewish leader late in life.

In fact, in his later years this man came to identify so strongly with the Jewish people that at times his own family took a back seat to his Jewish community service work. He became a prolific Jewish writer, a courageous activist, and an impressive community organizer. He was an insider-outsider of the Jewish people, and yet a remarkable leader. It may be that his multicultural experience of the world helped give him some useful perspectives on Jewish problems that made him more creative and effective as an advocate and agent of social change. In fact, the Jewish people have been permanently and profoundly influenced to the core by his life's work.

I'm speaking, of course, about Moses.

Opening my Yom Kippur sermon this way was incredibly fun. I got to look out at the congregants as I kept adding details about the man I was describing to them, and as I went on I could see some of them smiling, having figured it out partway through, and others leaning forward in their seats, curious to know which member of the congregation had led this

---

4. I'm referring here to the Jewish Federation. In every major metro area of the United States, there is an umbrella organization that serves Jewish community needs such as social work, the needs of the elderly, immigrant needs, poverty, and support for Israel.

checkered life of high drama. Of course, I was using an old public speaking technique—defamiliarizing the familiar—and I did it with a purpose.

I was pretty sure my congregants would benefit from looking at Moses as an outsider. Many of them see themselves as marginal Jews, outsiders to the tradition. Among the many non-Jewish members of the congregation there are also feelings of uncertainty about just where they fit in the Jewish community, or even if they have a place. The more I considered Moses' story—his early life growing up in the Pharaoh's court, his confusion over what his relationship was exactly to his enslaved ethnic brethren—the more I began to see Moses as a figure of astonishing relevance to twenty-first-century Jews (at least, those one finds outside the Orthodox world and especially among the ranks of the "unaffiliated," the growing number of Jews who choose not to belong to any synagogue). His mixed cultural background also makes him surprisingly relevant outside the contemporary Jewish community. Moses is worth reexamining in this era of cultural hybridization and globalization, an era that has produced a President of France with a Hungarian last name and a biracial American president who grew up in Indonesia and bears a Kenyan name.

The closer we look at the story of Moses in the Torah, the more we see of his experiences as an outsider to the Jewish people. It's not just that he was raised by the Pharaoh's daughter among Egypt's elites. Even his name didn't sound Hebrew to the slaves he sought to free. The Torah states that Pharaoh's daughter gave him the name "Moses," meaning "drawn from the water," commemorating her experience of finding him in a basket floating on the Nile. The Princess gave him that name in *her* language, ancient Egyptian, not Hebrew. (In fact, many scholars believe it comes from the ancient Egyptian "mos," meaning "child," or "son," as in "the royal names Thutmoses and Ramoses."[5]) The name "Moses" ultimately would become the single most popular Jewish boys' name, but when it first was given to the baby who would go on to lead the Hebrews to freedom, there was nothing Hebrew sounding about it. So when Moses shows up for the first time announcing to the Hebrew slaves that God has sent him to confront Pharaoh and bring about their liberation, they see a guy whose accent and mannerisms, as well as his name, identify him as Egyptian patrician. If this story were taking place today, it'd be like having the prophet sent by God to save the Jews be named "Mary Ann" or "Kareem." People would

5. Auerbach, *Moses*, 17.

have to get over their resistance to even saying the leader's name because of its associations with the distrusted Other. (Think of how the far right wing in the United States continues to express revulsion over President Barack Obama's name, often emphasizing his Arabic middle name, Hussein.) As if anticipating discomfort from religious traditionalists over the non-Hebrewness of Moses' name, the early twentieth-century Bible scholar Elias Auerbach wrote, "We have to acknowledge that the hero of the people Israel bears a non-Israelite name."[6]

But why is this difficult for any of us, traditionalists or otherwise, to acknowledge? My sense is that the Torah *intends* for us to think about the ethnic foreignness of Moses' name as a key lesson of the exodus story, so that we realize that real liberation requires stretching outside our comfort zones. To become free people, an act of trust in the unfamiliar was needed by the Hebrew slaves, and Moses had to work a long time to win that trust. Perhaps the Torah is showing us how something outside a tradition enters in, gains its place, and then becomes a new central element inside, so that we will remain open to this possibility and welcome it when it serves a higher purpose. As Auerbach observes, "Precisely [Moses'] intermediate position, his Israelite origin as well as his Egyptian education and culture, qualify him for the great work of liberation."[7] Martin Buber concurs:

> . . . in order that the one appointed to liberate his nation should grow up to be the liberator . . . he has to be introduced into the stronghold of the aliens, into that royal court by which Israel has been enslaved; and he must grow up there. This is a kind of liberation which cannot be brought about by anyone who grew up as a slave, nor yet by anyone who is not connected with the slaves; but only by one of the latter who has been brought up in the midst of the aliens and has received an education equipping him with all their wisdoms and powers, and thereafter "goes forth to his brethren and observes their burdens" [Exod 2:3].[8]

In fact, to push the point further, one could argue that the Torah intends for its readers to see not only Moses but the entire experience of Israelite slavery in Egypt as one in which cultural hybridization played an essential role in the formation of this group of semi-nomadic Hebrews

6. Ibid.

7. Ibid., 25.

8. Buber, *Moses: The Revelation and the Covenant*, 35.

into a new nation. To quote Buber again, "According to the Biblical account the entry of the Children of Israel in Egypt, and their departure 430 years later, were brought about by two Egyptianized Israelites."[9] Buber is referring to Joseph, from the book of Genesis, as the other cultural hybrid—the other "Egyptianized Israelite" besides Moses.[10] He points out that the Torah's telling of the saga of Israelite enslavement uses Joseph and Moses as "bookends" to the entire story, a literary technique that Bible scholars recognize as a signal of important information. Buber continues, "[Joseph and Moses] had both been accepted in Pharaoh's court, one as Grand Vizier and the other as the adopted son of a princess; and both had received Egyptian names, one from a King, the other from a King's daughter. The narrative stresses the connection between the two when it relates how at the Exodus Moses himself brought forth the bones of Joseph . . ."[11] We are who we are in part because of whom we encounter. We learn from others, even our oppressors, and we grow into ourselves in relationship with the Other.

***

In Moses' final moments, described in the last chapters of Deuteronomy, he remains ever the outsider, unable to participate in the Hebrews' main project, entering the Promised Land. Hundreds of thousands of anonymous Israelites will cross the Jordan River and settle in the Land of Israel, but Moses will not, ever. Not even once, just for a brief tour. The geographical boundaries of the Land of Israel represent a physical barrier that Moses forever remains outside of.

Moses pleads at one point with God, asking to be allowed just to take a quick journey through the different regions of the sacred land that will become the slaves' new home. But God sternly rejects him, and instead places Moses in the physical place of an outsider looking in.[12] He directs Moses to the top of a butte, from which he can see the land from a distance. We're so used to this part of Moses' life story that we often forget how astonishing this is. The central hero of the Jewish mythic tradition

9. Ibid., 20.

10. The biblical story of Joseph can be found in Gen 37–50.

11. Buber, *Moses: The Revelation and the Covenant*, 20.

12. Deut 34:1–4.

never in his entire life sets foot in the Land of Israel! In this respect, every Jew who has ever taken even the most generic tour-group trip to Israel is more of an insider to an essential part of the Jewish experience than Moses.

In yet another respect, Judaism has also left Moses on the margins. Sometimes a great person becomes deeply embedded within a tradition by way of his or her offspring, founding a lineage that goes on to shape part of the tradition's character over the generations. Yet, little of great renown comes of Moses' family line, in terms of privilege or fame among the generations of Jews to follow him. The book of Exodus tells us that Moses and his Midianite wife, Tzipporah, had two sons, Gershom and Eliezar. But neither one of them assumes Moses' position of leadership after his death. That distinction passes to Moses' faithful (and unrelated) assistant, Joshua, who leads the Hebrews into the Promised Land after Moses has died.

Consider this: Moses' brother, Aaron, becomes the father of a priestly lineage that carries forward in Jewish ritual life to this day (Jews bearing last names like Cohen, Cohn, Kahn, etc., trace their ancestry back to the ancient priesthood begun by Aaron and his sons). In contrast, Moses' lineage fades. Though he is also of the priestly tribe of Levi and though some priestly families are traced back to Moses, his renown as the father of an ongoing priestly lineage pales in comparison to Aaron's. Why? The other towering heroic figure of the Hebrew Bible, King David, sires a lineage that carries forward through generations of Israelite royalty. And David continues on in the religious imagination of the Jewish people as the famed ancestor of the promised Messiah that traditional Jews hope will arrive soon, ushering in an era of harmony and peace on earth once and for all. With Moses, we don't find many instances of later generations of Jewish leaders claiming to be his direct descendants in the same way that we do with David.

In the ancient Near East, lineage was precious. Through posterity, a person had a hope for some kind of immortality. That is why God's key promise to Abraham in Genesis is that he will become the father of multitudes. Given Abraham and Sarah's infertility well into their old age, God's offer of a great lineage is the most generous and loving thing God can offer these humble servants. Much of the drama and suspense of Genesis' stories about Abraham revolves around the question of whether God will ever make good on this promise. Once Abraham does become a father—first through Sarah's handmaiden, Hagar, and later through Sarah—then the suspense shifts to the question of whether each of the two precious sons will survive. Both sons face grave peril before the question is settled. The firstborn, Ishmael, is banished along with his mother, Hagar, into the harsh desert wilderness, with God's approval, as Abraham stands helplessly by. Though Hagar and Ishmael's prospects for survival are dim, God asks Abraham to trust that God will miraculously see to Ishmael's survival and to his eventual fathering of multitudes. Later, the second born son, Isaac, is nearly killed as a sacrificial offering by Abraham in God's famous test of the great patriarch's loyalty. In the end, however, Abraham dies knowing that God has kept the covenantal promise of lineage.

How curious then that Moses doesn't leave a lineage that carries a place of prominence in Judaism. It's yet another way that the tradition views him as an outsider and holds him at a certain distance even though he is, in many respects, as "inside" as one could be.

The early rabbis who studied and interpreted the Torah also saw elements of the outsider in Moses. Two closely related types of rabbinic interpretive literature of the Hebrew Bible are known as *midrash* and *aggadah*. In the rabbinic imagination, Moses is at times depicted as a stranger to the deeper meaning of the very Torah he is supposed to have written directly from God's dictation at Mount Sinai. In one famous example of aggadah, Moses finds himself in the uncomfortable position of the outsider who doesn't understand what's going on in a discussion of the Torah.

The scene is an ancient academy—a *yeshivah*—in which the great sage, Rabbi Akiva, is teaching his disciples. Granting Moses the miraculous opportunity to travel far into the future and witness a rabbinic giant interpreting the Torah, God zaps Moses instantaneously into Akiva's classroom. When he arrives, Moses finds himself seated in the back (the seven chairs in the front were reserved for the best students, and it's noteworthy that Moses is placed behind all of them). He sees Akiva expounding on the legal intricacies of a complex aspect of Jewish law in classic Talmudic fashion.

The Talmud, completed more than fifteen hundred years after Moses' lifetime, takes Jewish law in many far-flung directions that someone who had studied only the Torah—and none of the later rabbinic discussions of it—would scarcely recognize. In this instance, Moses listens carefully to the rabbi's lecture and finds himself completely baffled and anxious. Finally, one of Akiva's students asks the master how he arrived at a certain legal formulation. Akiva responds simply, "from the Law that Moses received at Mount Sinai." Although Moses doesn't understand Akiva's teaching, upon hearing that it is all being connected back to Torah, he feels relieved.[13] In this aggadah, Moses not only has the experience of being an outsider in a yeshivah, but he is confronted with the divinely ordained plan that the Jewish legal tradition bearing his name will be given over to others who will take it in directions that he can't imagine, that he will remain outside of.

***

For Jews who went to Hebrew school during their childhoods, the image of Moses the outsider is not one we encountered. I am told by Christian friends that the same has been true in Christian Sunday schools. The main images that religious school teachers, rabbis, and preachers emphasize are of Moses the faithful servant of God, Moses raising up his staff to split the Sea of Reeds,[14] and Moses saying, "Let my people go." Similarly, we are often taught about Moses during one of his intimate encounters with God—receiving the call from God at the burning bush; writing the words of the Torah down as God speaks them to him atop Mount Sinai; or going into the Tabernacle (in Hebrew, the *mishkan*) to meet with God. We also often hear about Moses reprimanding a rebellious and fickle Israelite nation in the wilderness, smashing the tablets of the Ten Commandments when he sees the Hebrews worshiping the golden calf, and warning the people not to stray from God's decrees. We are taught about Moses the lawgiver, but not Moses the intermarrier (more on this in chapter 4). Our religious schools emphasized Moses the prophet, not Moses the guy with the foreign sounding name and the strange lisp.

Yet we have so much to learn from Moses the outsider. To illustrate, here's how I continued with that Yom Kippur sermon:

13. BT Menachot 29b.

14. The body of water that is usually referred to as the Red Sea in the book of Exodus is actually not the Red Sea. In Hebrew it is called *yam suf*, which means "Sea of Reeds." Where exactly the Sea of Reeds was on the map is a point of ongoing debate among religious interpreters and historians alike.

Moses' life is a classic story of an outsider who becomes a crucial leader and a catalyst for change. He began his life with only the sketchiest awareness of being a Jew, and yet later he became actively involved in the life of his people. [Some years ago] I spoke [to this congregation] about the importance of diversity within the Jewish community, and I talked about how so many of us today are insider-outsiders of the Jewish people. Many of us, like Moses, have important parts of ourselves that have been nurtured outside the world of Judaism. Many of us have family who are not Jewish—like Moses with his Egyptian adoptive mother and his Midianite wife and influential father-in-law. If you are someone who happens to engage Jewish life minimally, I invite you to think about the fact that that's something Moses shared in common with you for a good part of his life.

In our sibling religion, Christianity, ministers often teach their congregants to try to emulate the life of their prophetic leader. It's interesting that Judaism doesn't really mirror that practice. Traditional Judaism has for centuries taught Jews to be faithful to God and perform the *mitzvot* [commandments] that God revealed to Moses, but the message in the synagogues and Hebrew schools hasn't been "try to be more like Moses." In fact, there's a well-known Hasidic tale in which a sage explains that when a person dies and goes to the afterlife, God does not ask them, "In your life on earth, why were you not more like Moses," but rather, God asks, "Why were you not more like yourself?"[15]

What I'd like to suggest is that in our era of culturally hybridized life—and we are all cultural hybrids—we are now living in a moment when many of us can start looking at Moses as a personal role model, but not in a way that traditional Judaism would have imagined a few centuries ago. Just as Moses spent much of his life outside the Jewish community, and just as Moses had many issues that put him outside the mainstream of Judaism (his criminal history, his disability, his intermarrying), so too many of us in this room have led somewhat wandering Jewish lives. What Moses' life can model for today's Jewish wanderers is the idea that every Jew who has lived at a distance from Jewish life for any part of their lives can choose to enter into the Jewish community and bring their wisdom, values, talents and ideals to bear upon Judaism. Judaism evolves and is influenced by people who give it their energy and creativity, and some of those people—like Moses—spend a part of their lives outside the Jewish world.

15. Buber, *The Way of Man*, 10. I have paraphrased the quote by Zusya of Hanipoli, an early Hasidic rabbi, which appears in Buber's book.

So if you're a twice-a-year Jew,[16] or if you're carrying the baggage of a bad childhood synagogue or Hebrew school experience, or if you're comfortable with one aspect of Judaism but stand at a great distance from other aspects, here's my message: We need you. We need you in this Jewish community, and we want you to bring all of yourselves—your experiences in other spheres, your ideals, your values, your questions, your passions and hopes. The Judaism that's going on in [our congregation][17] and in other liberal synagogues is a Judaism that welcomes you and offers you the opportunity to find meaning and create community. It needs active participants with new questions, new quarrels, new experiences and complex lives to reach its highest potential. Our tradition's greatest prophet was an outsider before he became an insider. He set the precedent for today's Jewish outliers to become participants in the ongoing evolution of our tradition. To all you Jews who have wandered or are wandering now, [this synagogue] is the kind of place that says, "you belong."

***

Moses as outsider, or perhaps more accurately as "outsider-insider," presents each of us with a model for taking part in—or even giving leadership to—a community that we may feel conflicted about or that we may count as only one of several of our communities of meaning. Most of us have our feet planted in more than one cultural setting, more than one community of meaning. Moses helps us integrate the perspectives we gain from the various communities of meaning of which we are a part, and bring them as gifts to the community we call home. There's a productive, creative perspective that outsider-insiders often have to offer. Who knows how much Moses may have learned as an Egyptian that ended up enhancing and benefiting the Israelites he went on to lead?

As many of the world's religious communities retreat into fundamentalism in response to anxiety about our rapidly interconnecting world, there is a great risk that growing intolerance will push outsider-insiders away. I worry that people who are moved by the goodness within their

16. "Twice-a-year Jew" is an expression used in the synagogue world to refer to Jews who come to synagogue only two times a year, on Rosh Hashanah, the Jewish New Year, and on Yom Kippur, the Day of Atonement.

17. The congregation I served at the time I gave this sermon—Temple Beth Israel in Eugene, Oregon.

religion, but who value insights from other religions or question certain elements of their own traditions, will simply opt out of their religions rather than stay involved and seek to contribute as outsider-insiders. If the outsider-insiders all leave the various religious communities of society, then the religious ground will all be ceded to those who find existential security in dogma and rigidity. Religions will then lose their ability to welcome ambiguity and their capacity to build connections between peoples. Moses teaches us that religion finds its spark, and perhaps its ability to be a force for positive transformation in the world, when people with a foot in and a foot outside play an important part in the religious community.

2

The Women Who Saved Moses

Civil Disobedience and the Seeds of Redemption

RARELY IS CIVIL DISOBEDIENCE given the emphasis it deserves in our tellings of the story of Moses. And yet it played a huge role in facilitating the
exodus from Egypt. Because of civil disobedience, specifically on the part
of several women, Moses survived his infancy and had the chance to lead
the Hebrew slaves to freedom.

As you may recall from the first chapter of Exodus, because the
Pharaoh feared the swiftly growing population of the Hebrews, he ordered
that the slaves' midwives murder all the male Jewish babies that they delivered.[1] The implication is that the midwives would be able to make the
deaths look like stillbirths—otherwise there would be no reason to order
the midwives to carry out the order of infanticide when soldiers could do
it easily, and without the need to try to arrive at each household at the moment of birth. Perhaps the midwives were expected to strangle the baby
boys as they helped them come through the birth canal. Perhaps Pharaoh
hoped that the Hebrews would come to think that the epidemic of stillbirths was some sort of plague from Egypt's gods or even from Pharaoh
himself, given that he claimed to be divine as well.

1. Exod 1:15–16.

But the midwives, led by their leaders, two women named Shifra and Puah, refused to carry out the order. They didn't announce their refusal. They just didn't kill the baby boys. When Pharaoh learned that his order was not being implemented, he summoned Shifra and Puah to account for this apparent insubordination. Thinking fast, they lied to Pharaoh about why his policy was failing. They told him that the Hebrew women are like animals, giving birth so quickly that by the time the midwives would arrive at the slaves' homes, the women would already have given birth.

Not only do Shifra and Puah tell a convincing and successful lie, but in telling their tale the Torah offers its readers a juicy literary moment. The midwives use the Hebrew words *ki-chayyot hey-nah*[2] to tell Pharaoh that the Hebrew women "are like animals," giving birth quickly. For the reader of Torah, the joke is on Pharaoh, because *chayyot*, the Hebrew word for "animals," creates a clever double entendre. *Chayyot* comes from the Hebrew root that means "life."[3] Reading between the lines, *ki-chayyot hey-nah* can also be understood to mean that the Hebrew women are full of *life*, even insinuating that they are *producers* of life, in defiance of the royal decree. As they fool the Pharaoh by pretending to disdain the Hebrew women, Shifra and Puah send the readers of Torah a little wink on the side. They've wrapped a seedling of life inside words of deception.

The closer we look at Shifra and Puah, the more fascinating they become. For instance, according to a plain reading of the biblical text, it is not clear whether Shifra and Puah, and all the midwives under their supervision who broke the Pharaoh's law, are Hebrews themselves.[4] The Hebrew that the Torah uses to describe the midwives is ambiguous: *meyaldot ha-ivriyot*.[5] Literally, this can mean "the midwives to the

2. Exod 1:19

3. Hebrew is a language of word families based on three letter roots, with a few exceptions. As a result, one of the most common ways a writer can convey multiple meanings is by selecting a Hebrew word whose root points to a secondary meaning. There are countless examples of this kind of literary play in the Hebrew Bible.

4. Numerous Torah commentators have noted this fact, including Burton L. Visotzky in *The Road to Redemption*, 41.

5. Exod 1:15. In midrash, the creative interpretive literature of the ancient rabbis, the claim is made that Shifra and Puah were actually Moses' mother and sister, Yocheved and Miriam. While this interpretive tradition yields its own richness, it is not an interpretation that is evident through a plain reading of the Torah text. Rashi, the French medieval Torah scholar, presents this midrashic tradition in his commentary on the midwives. However, not all of the classic Torah commentators share this view. Don Isaac Abravanel (1437–1508) comments about Shifra and Puah, "They were Egyptian women who were

Hebrews" or "the Hebrew midwives." To quote the Bible scholar Judy Klitsner, "[The Torah] deliberately withholds any definitive ethnic marking of these women. Had the text chosen to be explicit, it could have used an adjectival form of the term *benei Yisrael* (children of Israel), the designation used throughout the story [instead of the term *meyaldot ha-ivriyot*] . . . They were midwives of either Hebrew or Egyptian lineage."[6]

On the one hand, it's possible that Pharaoh would have had Hebrew women serving as midwives to their own kind. On the other hand, Pharoah may have commissioned midwives from some other ethnic group to facilitate and keep records of the slave births. In totalitarian systems like the one the Hebrew slaves would have lived under the authorities often seek control over many aspects of peoples' lives. Having a separate class of midwives to service the slaves would have given Pharaoh a powerful kind of leverage over slave families, given the uncertainty and danger of giving birth in the ancient world. Pharaoh would have thought of Shifra, Puah, and their crew of midwives as skilled technicians in a sort of animal husbandry, given the subhuman status of the slaves. The biggest hint the Torah offers that Shifra and Puah were not Israelites comes from the moment that the two midwives tell Pharaoh that their crew has failed to carry out his orders to kill the baby boys because "the Hebrew women are like animals." This appeal to Pharaoh's racism sounds like it is coming from people that he would have expected to share his subhuman perception of the Hebrews.

Why does it matter that the midwives who defied Pharaoh's orders might not be Hebrews? Because their act of refusal is the beginning of the revolution that ultimately frees the slaves. It's the exodus story's equivalent of the Shot Heard Round the World. We can't gloss over the fact that the midwives' civil disobedience is the first act of defiance against the Pharaoh's laws—against his whole system of authority—recorded in the Torah. If that act was done not by Israelites, but by people acting as allies to Israelites, then it teaches us how absolutely essential allies are for Jews—or any group facing oppression—when it comes to fighting for

---

midwives for the Hebrews; how could Pharaoh expect Hebrew women to kill Hebrew babies?" This is one of those cases in which I prefer the Torah's ambiguity to the midrashic tradition's creative new claims. English translation of Abravanel's comment taken from Michael Carasik's *The JPS Miqra'ot Gedolot: Exodus*.

6. Klitsner, *Subversive Sequels in the Bible*, 58.

freedom and dignity. It may be that the act of standing up for someone else is the necessary trigger for redemption on a grand scale.

Another crucial fact: this act of civil disobedience is done by women who act out of conscience. The language the Torah uses to describe their motivation is that they had "fear of God," which we might restate in a contemporary idiom as "tremendous awe for a higher moral authority." Rabbi Burton L. Visotzky calls this fear of God "what we would identify as moral courage."[7] Shifra and Puah and the midwives they lead chose to break Pharaoh's law in order to honor a higher law. They don't protest, picket, or chant slogans against Pharaoh's policy, but when push comes to shove they refuse to carry it out. They choose noncooperation. This was an enormous risk. They gambled with their lives doing this.

The midwives didn't know that they were planting the seeds for a chain of events that would defeat the mightiest empire on the face of the earth, free a people from four centuries of miserable slavery, and set in motion the birth of a new religion that would spawn several other religions and end up having global reach. They didn't know what they were setting in motion with their acts of courage. They simply had tremendous awe for a divine truth that they could not violate. Their fear of betraying this truth was greater than their fear of Pharaoh and his ability to imprison, torture, or kill them. Perhaps the Torah places their act of civil disobedience *first* in the story of the exodus because, in fact, they were midwives in more than one respect. They facilitated the birth not only of Hebrew babies, but also of the slave rebellion that would come, setting in motion the chain of events that would eventually lead to the emergence of the Abrahamic/monotheistic religions—all of this springs from their act of civil disobedience.

***

As the Torah tells the story, once the Pharaoh realized that his initial order to the midwives didn't work, he issued a new infanticidal order. All newborn Hebrew boys were to be taken from their parents and flung into the waters of the Nile to drown. Unlike the first order, which involved an attempt to conceal the murders during the hazards of birth, in order to carry out this order Pharaoh probably needed troops to patrol the Hebrew

7. Visotzky, *The Road to Redemption*, 43.

neighborhoods and take the babies by force from their weeping parents. When baby Moses is born, his mother, Yokheved, hides him for as long as she is able to get away with it—three months. But then, realizing that it is hopeless for her to try to keep his existence secret any longer, she commits the second act of civil disobedience recorded in the book of Exodus.

Working with her daughter, Miriam, she takes a basket and makes it watertight with slime and mud. She places her infant son in the basket and has Miriam go down to the Nile River, to an area where reeds grow thick, and set the basket afloat upon the waters. Pharaoh's law was to have the babies drowned in the Nile. Yokheved and Miriam defy this order by casting the baby boy off in a little life raft, hoping that someone from another segment of Egyptian society will find him and adopt him.

As we know, the tactic works. Miriam tracks the basket as it floats into the part of the river that flows near the Pharaoh's court. There, the Pharaoh's daughter is bathing with her maidens. When she sees the basket, she sends her maidens to bring it to her. "And she opened it, and saw the child; and look—a boy crying. And she had compassion on him, and said, 'This is one of the Hebrews' children.'"[8]

Her compassion led her to commit the third act of civil disobedience in the opening chapters of the book of Exodus. The daughter of the king who issued the murderous decree chooses to keep the child alive. Young Miriam, using her wits, bravely approaches the princess and cleverly asks, "Shall I go and get one of the Hebrew women to nurse the baby for you?"[9] When the princess answers yes, the whole episode turns into a joke at the Pharaoh's expense. Not only is the baby reunited with his mother for the next couple of years so he can be nursed, but Yokheved is paid the fees of a professional nursemaid for nursing her own baby![10]

We will examine the implications of the civil disobedience of the Pharaoh's daughter in detail in chapter 3, but for now let's just note that the princess has just taken her place in a series of acts of legal noncooperation that each proved essential for the entire story of the Jewish people to take place. And so far, each one of these acts of civil disobedience has been carried out by women. Moses' success owes everything to them. The risks they took were tremendous. They were motivated by conscience, love, and

8. Exod 2:6 *FOX*.
9. Exod 2:7 *NIV*.
10. Exod 2:9.

compassion, and they were women of action. As Reverend John Bell, a minister of the Church of Scotland, writes, "We discover that [Moses] owes a lot to women. He would not be alive had five women not defied male authority to allow him to exist. The women are two midwives, his mother, his sister, and Pharaoh's daughter."[11] Judy Klitsner puts it beautifully:

> Although Israel's savior is male, it is women who give him life and who see to his safety, sustenance, and upbringing. In addition, the selfless women in Moses' young life give birth to the independence of mind that will allow him to assume his role as leader. From them, Moses learns to examine the norms and values of his environment and to reject the corruption he sees among Egyptian and Israelite alike . . . [T]he daughters in this narrative lead Moses to an awareness of his otherness, and ultimately to a discovery of the heroism needed to conceive of and carry out the move to redemption. If we are to trace a line from the midwives to Moses, we find that time after time the solitary stature of courageous, conscience-driven individuals has paved the way to godliness.[12]

***

The Torah's intent to call attention to these women is clear. Shifra, Puah, Yokheved, Miriam, and the Pharaoh's daughter each take center stage and drive the plot's action in their respective scenes in the text. By the time we reach the point in the book of Exodus when all three of these acts of civil disobedience have taken place, the only men involved in the story have been passive figures. One of these men, the Pharaoh, does play the active role of issuing decrees, but he is passively limited to waiting for reports about his orders from the field, and he ends up being an impotent king whose orders are twice circumvented. He is also easily deceived by Shifra and Puah. The other two males in the story thus far are Moses' father, who appears nowhere in the Torah's telling of the placing of baby Moses in the basket on the Nile, and of course baby Moses himself, who is completely helpless throughout.

So here we have a Torah tradition that emphasizes two crucial elements of revolutionary action on behalf of social justice: civil disobedience and women's creative defiance of unjust authority. It's right there in

11. John Bell, excerpted from the BBC's "Moses" article on the religion section of their Web site. http://www.bbc.co.uk/religion/religions/judaism/history/moses_1.shtml.

12. Klitsner, *Subversive Sequels in the Bible*, 62.

the text, written in dramatic and very active language, and yet it's generally underemphasized in Western tellings of the Moses story. Thankfully,
this has begun to change. In recent years, some feminist Bible scholars,
traditional commentators, and other teachers have been calling attention
to these heroic women of the exodus story. For example, the editors of the
new Passover Haggadah of the Reconstructionist movement have added
the following passage to the beginning of the Passover seder's telling of the
story of the Hebrews' liberation from Egypt:

> We begin our story with the first stirrings of freedom. How was
> the desire for freedom first aroused? By the midwives, Shifrah and
> Puah, who resisted Pharaoh's decree . . . By Miriam, who watched
> over her brother Moses to insure his safety. In the face of death,
> they advocated life. In the birth waters and in the Nile, these ex-
> traordinary women saw life and liberation . . .[13]

Thanks to creative liturgical efforts like this one, the brave women of
the exodus are starting to be less overlooked.

One thing is clear: it's not the way the Torah presents the story that
has led us to tend to gloss over the crucial themes of civil disobedience
and the valor of smart and brave women in the story of Moses' life. As
Burton Visotzky writes, "The biblical book of Exodus displays a keen
consciousness of the enormity of women's roles in keeping the people of
Israel alive . . . [T]he Bible itself leads the way, clearly recognizing women
not merely as wives and mothers but as partners in affecting the redemption of the Jews."[14] The reason for the scanty attention we've paid these
women in modern synagogues and churches lies with our own culturally
determined tendency to focus instead on the men in the story and on the
other forms of resistance to Pharaoh's oppression that grab our attention
later in the exodus drama, such as the direct confrontations Moses and
Aaron ultimately have with Pharaoh, the ten plagues, the parting of the
Sea of Reeds, and so on. All of those are also important elements of the
slave rebellion and escape, but the whole story begins with—and hinges
on—the civil disobedience of multiple women, some Jewish, some not;
some poor, and some very close to the seat of power.

13. Levitt and Strassfeld, *A Night of Questions—A Passover Haggadah,* 35.
14. Visotzky, *The Road to Redemption,* 84.

3

Mother of Moses, Princess of Egypt

And she opened it, and saw the child; and look—a boy crying. And she had
compassion on him, and said, "This is one of the Hebrews' children."
—Exod 2:6, *FOX*

IN THE BRIEF MOMENT described by the verse above, as the daughter of the
most powerful emperor in the world stood face to face with an abandoned
Hebrew baby boy condemned to die by her father's order, the seed of the
overthrow of four centuries of slavery was planted. In the time it took for
one young woman's heart to feel a pulse of compassion strong enough
to evoke action, the gods of Egypt fell, and the God of Israel entered the
drama of history on the world's stage as the Champion of the Oppressed.
Rameses II, if he was the Pharaoh of the book of Exodus, as many scholars
suppose, had no idea that his undoing would be plotted within his own
court, by his own flesh and blood. The revolution was born in the most
unlikely of places—inside his unnamed daughter's heart.

This is how it happened: there was a chance meeting that Rameses
couldn't have anticipated, an accidental encounter between a royal princess and a Hebrew infant, and the spontaneous rising up of a feeling in a
single human being—"and she had compassion on him," as the text says.
The Pharaoh had built up a seemingly invincible structure of unchal-
lengeable power, a system of total dominance that oppressed millions and

had no serious rivals. And yet there was a crack in it at the highest levels that his system of absolute power couldn't control or predict.

This part of the story of Moses—the story of his adoptive mother's compassion and subversion—teaches us yet another lesson that is rarely taught in Sunday school. It's an ancient observation about the vulnerabilities of absolute power structures in human societies. Even if they are seemingly invincible, these power structures have cracks in them, even at the highest levels. Poor Yokheved, baby Moses' biological mother, acted on the hope that this "crack" was part of reality. It was a desperate act. She dared to have faith that there was something more to the world than raw power and callousness. She cast her condemned son upon the waters of the Nile—the symbol of the life of all of Egypt—in the hope that someone, somewhere in this empire of cruelty might feel a stirring of sympathy and choose to rescue the child.

This part of the story of Moses' early life emphasizes the revolutionary message that even the mightiest empires can't kill the heart's unpredictable potential for a sudden blossoming of compassion. Love, compassion, even a sense of justice are eternal flames that cannot be extinguished, and this unforeseeable variable is what keeps hope alive in desperate times. Spontaneous and transformative moments of caring can't be fully stamped out by any system of power and control. Rabbi Abraham Joshua Heschel wrote about this kind of moment as "an impulse overwhelming the heart, usurping the mind; . . . a drive towards serving God who rings our hearts like a bell."[1] This is what makes tyrants insecure, and keeps even the most entrenched global structures of oppression uncertain.

Modern rabbis like Heschel and Michael Lerner have written eloquently about the revolutionary nature of the Torah's message, stressing that the epic story of the Hebrews is a story intended to inspire people to overturn all unjust power structures. As Rabbi Lerner writes:

> Throughout much of recorded history the oppressed have been socialized to believe that cruelty and oppression are inevitable, an ontological necessity, part of the structure of reality. Spirituality for them became identified with reconciliation to a world of oppression: either through learning to "flow" with the world as it is or through imagining that the material world in which they lived

1. Heschel, *Man Is Not Alone*, 174. I'd like to thank my teacher, Rabbi Nancy Fuchs-Kramer, for suggesting this quote from Heschel. I took the liberty of adapting Rabbi Heschel's words by changing the word "Him" to "God."

was a prelude to some higher non-material world, and that the task of the living was to escape material reality into this spiritual realm which embodied the purity and deeper reality that could not be imagined on this earth.

What the Jews heard was a very different message: that this world could be fundamentally transformed . . . The God of the Bible is the Force that makes possible this transformation of the world. Judaism becomes the metaphysics of social transformation: the system of belief about reality that makes possible revolutionary change . . . Human beings need not be stuck in a world of pain or oppression.[2]

The actions of the Pharaoh's daughter, the sudden turning in her heart the day she found that exposed baby—this is the revolutionary spirit of Torah in the microcosm of a single human heart.

Another thought: many commentators have noted that the book of Exodus never tells us the Pharaoh's name, and that this is somewhat surprising given how incredibly important the events that took place were in the history of the Israelites. The Torah only uses the terms "Pharaoh" and "King of Egypt." Later in the Hebrew Bible, the Assyrian and Babylonian emperors who attacked and oppressed the Israelites are named, but not this Pharaoh. We might wonder if this omission is the result of ignorance on the part of the Torah's authors or editors. But they certainly knew of figures like Rameses II, because the Torah states that one of the cities the slaves built was called Rameses. Some biblical interpreters have suggested that the reason the Torah only uses generic terms to refer to the Pharaoh is to stress the timeless and universal nature of the story. Resisting injustice, struggling for freedom, and hoping for the light to shine in through the cracks in the edifices of power are constants in the human experience, and history is full of Pharaohs.

***

The Torah never tells us the name of Pharaoh's daughter. The rabbis of midrash, however, gave her a name, and a mighty name at that. They called her "daughter of God"—*Batya* in Hebrew.[3] In giving her this name the rabbis offer us two wonderful reversals. The first is the more obvious

2. Lerner, *Jewish Renewal*, 26–29.
3. This Hebrew name corresponds to the English name, Beth.

one: her name proclaims that the daughter of Pharaoh has been "adopted" by the Hebrews' God as God's own daughter. In adopting the abandoned Hebrew baby she herself becomes adopted by Pharaoh's rival for true ultimate power in the world, God.

The second reversal is more complicated. In giving the Hebrew infant an Egyptian name, "Moses," the Pharaoh's daughter brought the Hebrew Other into Egyptian life. This illustrates another crack in Pharaoh's system of oppression. He didn't imagine or anticipate that, in enslaving the Hebrews, he would inevitably intertwine Egyptian and Hebrew life in ways that he could not foresee. The Law of Unintended Consequences strikes again. Pharaoh embraced the illusion of human control in a way that is consistent with the hubris that has led many powerful people to miscalculate the ultimate effects of their actions. Just as Pharaoh's daughter has given a Hebrew child an Egyptian name and altered the course of history, the rabbis give the Egyptian princess a Hebrew name. In naming she is named.

Furthermore, it's worth noting that both Batya and Moses must have had names prior to the ones by which we have come to know each of them through Torah and midrash, and yet we don't know what those names were. The Torah tells us that Moses' Hebrew mother hid him for three months before finally placing him in a basket and casting him out upon the Nile hoping for his rescue. Yokheved and Amram, the baby's parents, had their son for three months! They must have given him a name—a Hebrew name. We don't know what that name is because the Torah never mentions it.

Likewise, the Torah never tells us the name that the Pharaoh's daughter was given by her parents, which certainly wasn't Batya. Both Moses and Batya are *renamed* in the same instant, when light poured in through a crack in the Pharaonic system of oppression. Tyrants like Pharaoh have the power to name things, and they count on the names of things remaining stable, like the other objects of their control. What they can't control, however, is something the Torah shows us in this story: the unexpected events of our lives can change us utterly, even changing our names, renaming us into members of a counter-force to the system of oppression.

This part of the story of Moses teaches us that the seeding of a new era of history can happen in the brief moment it takes for a single person to have a change of heart. In that moment, when compassion stirs one person to the point of some small act of resistance to a system of evil, we witness an aspect of reality that no CEO, president, dictator, or Supreme Leader can eliminate from the human experience: compassion's version of the butterfly effect.

History has brought us the rise of one system of oppression after another, as well as countless human systems that are mixtures of good and evil. But no system of evil has been stable and fortified enough to last forever—and that is a comforting thought. And many have teetered and broken down at least in part because of compassion's butterfly effect.

In American mythology, Rosa Parks' refusal to give up her seat on a Jim Crow bus stands out in our collective consciousness as the pebble that started the avalanche towards racial equality. Of course, as many civil rights scholars have pointed out, Rosa Parks wasn't the first black person in Montgomery who had refused to give up her seat and gotten arrested for it. Nor was Parks a random person who had never gotten involved in the civil rights movement before that catalyzing moment on the bus. She was an officer in her local chapter of the NAACP. She also had trained for civil rights work, including preparing for possible civil disobedience, at the Highlander Folk Institute in Tennessee. She and many blacks and whites in her community had worked for years to change the system of segregation and white supremacy that had been in place literally for centuries. Her famous refusal to give up her seat on the bus wasn't a pre-planned action—it was a spontaneous decision resulting from her having simply had enough at a given moment. But her training and community organizing assuredly contributed to her decision to act on her feelings that particular day.

What we learn from Parks and the others in Montgomery who were well prepared to maximize the impact of her act of passive resistance is that well-organized, morally principled, and patient group work for social justice primes the pump for catalyzing moments to take place. Organizing a principled social change movement committed to using ethical means for just ends helps mobilize people effectively when an unexpected opportunity arises. The success of the 1955 Montgomery Bus Boycott teaches us that we should organize and ready ourselves for those moments when the inevitable cracks in unjust power structures begin to rupture, so that we can take advantage. The cracks are there. Preparation increases the odds that when light comes pouring through a small crack, people will be ready to widen that crack and let a wave of light rumble through.

The story of Batya teaches something perhaps even more hopeful. Unlike Rosa Parks, the Torah doesn't tell us that Batya had for years been secretly meeting with Egyptian abolitionists, or that she had been part of a political movement that helped prepare her for the kind of moment that came along when a Hebrew baby floated towards her on the waters of the Nile. Rather, the impression we get from the text is that Batya had most likely lived well within the privileged bubble of the royal court, and that her decision to rescue the Hebrew baby was a purely spontaneous act of compassion. The implication is that even without an organizing effort by a committed resistance movement, the System can't prevent all the possible things that can happen to undermine its grip on power. There really is a crack (or more likely, many cracks) in everything, and some of the cracks are close to the center of power. Try to control every human heart, to seal off the possibility of love weeding its way somehow to the surface—it's beyond any System's capacities of control.

4

Moses and Tzipporah

When Intermarriage Is Good for the Jews[1]

ALTHOUGH ATTITUDES TOWARDS INTERMARRIAGE within the Jewish community have moved in the direction of tolerance and acceptance over the last generation, mainstream Jewish institutions continue to treat intermarriage as a negative—one of the great costs of American freedom and its companion, assimilation. The big fear about Jewish intermarriage is that, as a people of very small numbers, we might marry ourselves out of existence. Flat population numbers and the hovering emotional legacy of the massive losses we experienced during the Nazi Holocaust exacerbate these fears. (There were eighteen million Jews before the Holocaust. Today there are about fifteen million. Sixty years later, we still haven't replenished the six million lives the Nazis took from us.) The fears are understandable, and it isn't surprising that Jewish leaders often discuss intermarriage in very negative terms, citing worrisome demographic studies and wondering what sorts of community programs will get more Jews to marry Jews. And yet, intermarriage is nothing new for Judaism. It's as ancient as the

1. Significant parts of this chapter first appeared in publication in an article I wrote called "Jews and Fellow Travelers: Appreciating the Gifts of Non-Jewish Partners."

Torah itself, and, interestingly, the Torah treats intermarriage with a wide range of attitudes.

Moses himself intermarried,[2] and the story of his marriage, and the benefits the Jewish people derived from his non-Jewish spouse and in-laws, are emphasized in the Torah. After fleeing Egypt and being welcomed warmly by the Midianite priest Jethro, Moses marries Tzipporah, Jethro's daughter. Ultimately, both Jethro and Tzipporah play integral roles in making Moses' Jewish journey possible. According to the contemporary Bible scholar Judy Klitsner, Jethro and Tzipporah also help Moses experience love, belonging, and a sense of family in ways he never had had before in his life, and this experience helped Moses grow in a way he needed to in order to become the leader he would one day be: "With his actions, Jethro begins to draw Moses out of his solitude . . . Moses feels relief and gratitude at ending his isolation . . . From the safety of Jethro's home, with his wife and son in tow, Moses looks back on his life in Egypt, the land of his two mothers and two nationalities, and of his vast but failed potential for kinship. Only now, in this new land of Midian, does Moses realize that until his meeting with the priest Jethro, he has been estranged from everyone."[3]

Later, Tzipporah helps Moses survive a brush with death in a mysterious passage in which she takes a lifesaving and active role in seeing to the Jewish religious requirement that their son be circumcised.[4] In this brief episode in which Moses and Tzipporah are on the road to Egypt, God suddenly appears to them at night and physically attacks Moses with seemingly murderous intent. Tzipporah quickly intervenes, circumcising their son, and confronts the Divine Being who has attacked Moses by presenting the skin and blood of the circumcision. The Being retreats

---

2. I make this assertion based on a simple reading of the biblical text. The Torah doesn't ever state that Tzipporah converted to Judaism (which would be complicated to define at the time Moses married her, since the Torah itself hadn't been given at Mount Sinai). Nevertheless, in midrash the ancient rabbis, perhaps alarmed at the Torah's silence on the question of Tzipporah's religious identity, proclaimed that Tzipporah became a convert. On this basis, many traditional Jews would argue that I'm incorrect in stating that Moses intermarried. In sticking purely with the biblical text, and differing with the midrashic tradition on this question, I'm choosing a reading of the biblical text that is absolutely plausible and, in my opinion, more helpful to the current questions facing the Jewish people.

3. Klitsner, *Subversive Sequels in the Bible*, 84–85.

4. Exod 4:24–26.

and Moses' life is spared. The passage is difficult to translate and includes confusing pronouns, so it's hard to say exactly what happened down to the detail. But Tzipporah's actions clearly have saved the day.

Some interpreters reason that since Tzipporah knew about the *mitz-vah*—the commandment—to circumcise, the Torah is hinting that she had in fact renounced the gods of Midian and "converted to Judaism," as it were. That's possible, but why would the Torah omit mentioning her "conversion" if it was so crucial to her taking the place of being Moses' wife?

Tzipporah's quick action to circumcise her son brings to mind something we rabbis often see in contemporary intermarriages: families in which the non-Jewish partner, especially the woman in a heterosexual marriage, is the one who becomes knowledgeable about Jewish traditions and takes the lead in ensuring they're being observed and passed on to children.[5] Perhaps what's happening in this circumcision story involving Tzipporah is an ancient version of the same dynamic—a non-Israelite wife who had learned about her husband's people and their traditions stepped up at a crucial moment to help him see through his religious obligations. This reading would be consistent with the book of Exodus' earlier theme of non-Israelite women taking supportive action to protect Moses and the Hebrews, as discussed in chapters 2 and 3 above. Whatever her reasons were for taking bold action during this strange encounter with God, we know this much about Tzipporah: this Midianite woman makes a gift of her love, devotion, encouragement, and support to the greatest prophet of Jewish tradition.

Let's turn back to Jethro, the Midianite priest who becomes Moses' father-in-law. In the mythic storytelling of the Torah, a great leader like Moses doesn't find rescue after fleeing the Egyptian authorities by *randomly* arriving at the encampment of a priest of Midian. The Torah presents Jethro's camp as the place God *chose* for Moses to come to, just as the Torah means for us to see God's hand guiding the basket carrying baby Moses on the waters of the Nile to the place where Pharaoh's daughter happened to be bathing. Moses' befriending of the Midianite holy man is no accident, nor is his marrying Tzipporah, a woman who not only was not Israelite herself, but who initially perceived Moses as an Egyptian, not

5. An organization called the Jewish Outreach Institute has done serious research on this particular phenomenon in heterosexual intermarried households in which the female partner is the non-Jewish spouse.

a Hebrew. It's a cross-cultural family system that takes root and flourishes at Jethro's compound near Mount Sinai in Midian, and it's in that kind of culturally integrated setting that Moses matured and became ready to receive God's call to return to Egypt and demand the release of the Hebrews.

Shortly after the exodus from Egypt, Jethro travels to visit his son-in-law and family members in the wilderness. He arrives at the Hebrews' camp and sees Moses struggling to resolve all the disputes among the Israelites. Putting his arm around Moses' shoulder, the priest of Midian tells him how to set up a system of courts and delegate the burden of judging.[6] The first Israelite judiciary system comes from a non-Israelite who joined a Hebrew family through his daughter's intermarriage. For intermarried couples today, Jethro can serve as an inspirational figure, exemplifying the fact that not only non-Jewish spouses, but non-Jewish family members can be important allies to the Jewish people.

Before I leave the subject of Jethro, I want to acknowledge a possible refutation some in the Jewish world might make to my depiction of Jethro as an example of a praiseworthy non-Jewish family member in the Torah. In classical midrash, the rabbis depict Jethro as a model convert, and therefore, from a traditional Jewish theological perspective, the story of Jethro is really the story of a righteous Jew-by-choice (similar to how the early rabbis assumed Tzipporah's conversion, as discussed above).

Rabbinic tradition cites Exod 18:10–11 as evidence of Jethro's conversion and abandonment of polytheism at this point in his life. In these verses, Jethro pays homage to Moses' God and declares that he now sees that the God of Israel is the greatest of all gods. But Jethro's statement doesn't necessarily imply his conversion (which, for the rabbis of midrash, would need to include a total repudiation of polytheism). In the ancient Near East, it's highly likely that a polytheistic Midianite like Jethro would blend and mix his religious practices. Read from this perspective, Jethro's proclamation of homage to the God of Israel informs us that he sees the God of Israel in a new light due to God's triumph over the gods of Egypt, and that he now places the God of Israel at the top of his personal pantheon. But even if the ancient rabbis are right and Jethro did abandon his worship of other gods from this point in the story forward, he still would have been a polytheist during the many years he was with Moses from the time he took him in until the time of the exodus. During those years

6. Exod 18:13–24.

he supported Moses as a loving father-in-law, encouraging Moses on his spiritual path and, most likely, teaching Moses in ways we can only imagine. However we choose to understand Exod 18:10–11, when we consider Jethro we can make the case that what the Torah is modeling in the story of Moses' life in Midian is that sometimes intermarriage is "good for the Jews."

I'm not suggesting that the Hebrew Bible speaks in only positive terms about intermarriages. Not at all. The multivocal Torah and the rabbinic tradition include many negative texts about intermarriage. As I've mentioned, in some cases, the rabbis "eliminated" apparent intermarriages in the Torah. They used midrash, the classic form of rabbinic interpretation of Torah, to convert Tzipporah, Jethro, and the Pharaoh's daughter to Judaism, although none of these conversions is mentioned in the Torah text itself. In the purely biblical account, however, Judaism's greatest leader was raised by a non-Jewish mother, intermarried when he grew up, and then sought counsel from his non-Jewish father-in-law. Although "Moses the intermarrier" is an image we never hear brought up in contemporary Jewish discussions of how to approach intermarriage, perhaps its time has come.

For a long time I have worried that, within the Jewish community, our current communal messages about intermarriage (by which I mean both heterosexual and homosexual partnerships) may be damaging our chances to respond to intermarriage in healthy and productive ways. And so, in 2004, when I was asked to participate in a Jewish convention workshop that would examine intermarriage from a perspective of appreciation, I readily said yes. Full disclosure: I myself was intermarried during part of my tenure as a rabbinical student, though my wife completed her conversion to Judaism before I was ordained. I was partly motivated to participate on this panel because of my own deeply felt convictions around this issue. The other three panelists were Jewish or non-Jewish partners in interfaith marriages who are seriously involved in synagogue life. Our goal was to challenge the *framework of costs* that the Jewish community typically applies to discussions of intermarriage: "How many Jews down the line will intermarriage cost us?"

Because of this framework of costs, the Jewish discussion of intermarriage is confined to a false debate between those who argue for less tolerance of intermarriage and more in-reach to "truly committed" (that is, non-intermarried) Jews, versus those who argue for more outreach to the intermarried to maximize their involvement in synagogue life. Both sides approach intermarriage as an unfortunate reality to be mitigated by either increased shunning or tactical welcoming. The idea that intermarriage may produce some *benefits* for the Jewish community—as it did in Moses' case—is rarely, if ever, included in the discussion.

In planning our panel, we made an effort to find a new name for non-Jews who are part of the Jewish community—a name that would express the complexity of their place as insider-outsiders. The term we came up with was "Fellow Travelers."[7] Fellow Travelers are non-Jews who, because of ties of love and friendship, are part of the Jewish community but are not necessarily en route to conversion (or, to use the preferred terminology, becoming Jews-by-choice[8]). Fellow Travelers accompany the Jewish community on its journey and sometimes take part in the evolution of Judaism.

Tzipporah was a Fellow Traveler who made enormous contributions to the survival and success of the Jewish people. Delilah was a Fellow Traveler who did not. What the Hebrew Bible presents is a portrait of intermarriage that sometimes highlights benefits, and sometimes warns of costs. Often in the Hebrew Scriptures, the attitude towards non-Israelite spouses is based on the content of their activity—their commitments to Israelite principles and to the success of the Israelites in difficult situations. Moses married a Midianite who learned about Moses' God, supported his work to free the Hebrew slaves and lead them in the wilderness, and made sure he took care to circumcise his son. She wasn't an Israelite, but she helped support and carry out Israelite obligations and she contributed to the well-being of the Israelites as a people. And as an Israelite who intermarried, Moses obviously went on to make huge contributions to the religion and culture of the Israelites.

---

7. Because this term was used during the McCarthy era to describe Communist sympathizers, we briefly considered searching further, but given the half-century that has passed since that usage, we felt that the name was worth redeeming.

8. "Jew-by-choice" is the preferred term, as opposed to "convert." There are complex reasons for this preferred terminology that have to do with the differences between a classical Christian conversion ("seeing the light" and choosing to embrace a particular theology) and the process of incremental study, experience, and acculturation involved in choosing to become a Jew and join the Jewish people as a "full citizen."

What we can learn today from Moses on the subject of Jewish inter-marriage is the need to recognize that it is a source of benefits as well as costs. Our communal adaptation should be one that seeks to recognize, maximize, and give thanks for the benefits that many non-Jewish spouses bring to the Jewish people at the same time that we try to minimize the costs of intermarriage. Moses ventured into the unknown and was open to the loving commitment of a human being who was willing to join him on a Jewish journey. She was Midianite and it all worked out well. For the Jewish people, my hope is that Moses' life story will become more deeply incorporated into the Jewish discussion of intermarriage, inviting us to look into the subject with more curiosity and less panic, more balance and less fear, more appreciation of true friends in our midst and less as-sumed negativity. Intermarriage is a complex phenomenon with costs and benefits, and it's here to stay. Moses needs to be a part of the conversation.

5

Moses and Jethro

Religion as a Creative Open System

IN CHAPTER 18 OF Exodus, Moses and the Israelites are encamped near Mount Sinai in the wilderness, having recently escaped Egyptian bondage once and for all. Jethro, Moses' Midianite father-in-law, last saw Moses as he was departing for Egypt on God's assignment to confront Pharaoh and free the slaves. Now the elderly Midianite priest journeys out to visit his victorious son-in-law. They meet and embrace in joy. Jethro listens as Moses recounts the entire story of the liberation. He offers praises to the God of Israel, and he shares a celebratory meal with Moses, Aaron, and all the elders, complete with offerings to God.

Here's what happens next:

> And so it was, the next day, that Moses sat to judge disputes for the people. And the people stood before Moses from morning until evening. And when Moses's father-in-law saw all that Moses was doing for the people, he said, "What is this thing that you're doing for the people? Why are you sitting by yourself, while the entire nation stands over you from morning until evening?"
>
> And Moses replied to his father-in-law, "Because the people come to me to seek out [the judgment of] God. When an issue emerges among them, it comes before me, and I judge between a

person and his or her neighbor. In so doing, I cause them to know the laws of God and God's teachings."

Then Moses' father-in-law said to him, "This is not good, this thing that you're doing! You will certainly wear out—both you and this people along with you! Because it's too heavy for you, this thing. You can't do it by yourself. Now listen to my voice. I'm going to give you some advice, and God be with you. You should be [stationed] between the people and God, so that you can bring these matters before God. And you should enjoin them regarding the laws and the teachings, and make them understand the way they should follow and the things they should do. However, you must assign from among all the people men of strength, who fear God—honest men who hate corruption. And you should install them as officials over thousands, officials over hundreds, officials over fifties, and officials over tens. And let them judge the people at all times of year. And every major matter they'll bring to you, but every minor matter they can judge. In this way, they'll lighten things for you and bear things along with you. If you do this thing, and God commands you so, then you'll be able to withstand; moreover, all of this people will be able to arrive in its place in peace." And Moses listened to the voice of his father-in-law, and he did all that he had said.[1]

As mentioned briefly in chapter 4 above, this scene depicts one of the crucial early formative moments of the Israelites' system of self-governance. Jethro, a non-Israelite—in fact, a priest of another religious tradition—provides Moses' people with its system of courts of law. Moses is open to receiving his input and advice, and he trusts that it is right for him to incorporate it into the emerging body of law and justice that this newly forming nation will have. Note that Moses and the Israelites receive, accept, and obey this *torah*—for the word "torah" means "teaching"—from a Midianite priest even *before* they receive the Torah (with a capital T) from God at Mount Sinai.

The creativity that led to the founding of the Hebrews' system of courts resulted from a combination of elements: the observations of a loving and concerned family member of a different religious tradition; the lack of egotism on the part of Moses, whose main concern was to do right by the people; and the openness of Moses and the Israelites themselves to acting upon a good and worthy idea that came from an outsider. This kind

1. Exod 18:13–24. Translation mine.

of adaptive and open-minded behavior characterizes what some in the scientific fields of chaos and complexity theory call a *creative open system*.

The physicist and chaos scientist F. David Peat and his coauthor John Briggs point us towards a definition of a creative open system by way of describing its opposite, a closed system or "limit-cycle system."[2] They write, "Limit-cycle systems are those that cut themselves off from the flux of the external world because a great part of their internal energy is devoted to resisting change and perpetuating relatively mechanical patterns of behavior."[3] Societies and religions that are organized with rigid walls defending them from outside influence, that seek to stifle the unknown and maximize uniformity and predictability within, are examples of limit-cycle systems in human affairs. Briggs and Peat describe political limit-cycle systems as societies that make people feel powerless, such as totalitarian regimes.[4]

In contrast, some societies have a swirl of internal activity going on expressing their unique, authentic personality, but at the same time their boundaries are permeable, and constructive ideas or influences from the outside are allowed to enter the system and become part of it. These societies operate as creative open systems. This is exactly what we see happening in Exodus 18.

When Jethro introduces a new legal structure—maybe even one he learned from Midianite tradition—and Moses absorbs it into the emerging religion of his people, we see a creative open system in action. The dynamism that sprang from the merging of Israelite law with a new idea from the outside caused the Israelite system to evolve. And rather than dilute the authenticity of the Israelites' legal system, Jethro's judiciary model actually strengthened the vitality of Israelite law because it required a large number of Israelites to become knowledgable enough about the laws of Torah to be able to adjudicate disputes.

Here's how Briggs and Peat describe a creative open system using the metaphoric image of a swirling vortex in nature, like the kind one might see in an ocean, river, or lake: "In a vortex, a constantly flowing cell wall separates inside from outside. However, the wall itself is both inside and outside. The same is the case for the membranes in animal and plant

2. Briggs and Peat, *Seven Life Lessons of Chaos*.
3. Ibid., 40.
4. Ibid.

cells."[5] Creative open systems, whether in biology or in human societies, have permeable membranes. Nutrients and supportive elements can come in. There is a boundary, a difference between Self and Other, and yet in some crucial ways Self and Other are interpenetrating and interdependent. In religious and cultural contexts, Briggs and Peat offer this image as well: "The importance of creative openness is reflected in the talking circle of the Blackfoot people. It is the organizational center of their community, the circle where they make their decisions, but they are always careful to leave a gap for the new to enter. This gap represents the open flow always present within their self-organization."[6]

***

In Exodus 18, we have a chance to learn from Moses that religions and nations function best as creative open systems. It's a notion that cuts completely against the common image we've been given of Moses as the stern lawgiver seeking to shut out the dangerous influences of the surrounding polytheists. For sure, those images are there in the Torah too, but they sit alongside Exodus 18 and other biblical examples that embrace a creative open system model.

Consider, for example, the reign of King Solomon a few hundred years after Moses' lifetime. When King Solomon set out to build the First Temple in Jerusalem, he turned to an outsider—a Phoenician King, Hiram—for help. Several chapters of 1 Kings and 2 Chronicles describe Solomon's written requests to Hiram to have his skilled Phoenician woodsmen chop down cedar trees and prepare them for shipment to Jerusalem so they could be used throughout the Temple, including in the most sacred room of all, the Holy of Holies.

Solomon also asked Hiram to provide him with a master craftsman with skill in bronze work, as well as knowledge of how to work with other precious metals, cloth, dyes, and engraving.[7] Hiram granted Solomon's request and selected a man called Huram, who was, interestingly enough, half-Israelite, half-Phoenician. Huram directed a mixed team of Israelites and Phoenicians in the craftsmanship and detailed work that resulted in

5. Ibid., 28.
6. Ibid., 27.
7. See 1 Kgs 7 and 2 Chr 4.

the creation of the sacred vessels of the Temple as well as many of its beautiful features.[8]

When the time came to build the holiest structure in all of Israelite history—the Temple in Jerusalem—King Solomon trusted in creative openness. He didn't reason that the Temple and its sacred vessels needed to be crafted and built solely by Israelites in order to protect some rigid notion of religious purity in this holiest of projects. He didn't decide that because Phoenician polytheists were idolaters, therefore their artistic and architectural ideas would pollute a "pure" monotheism that the Temple, after all, required. Not at all. He invited help from a neighboring civilization that knew a thing or two about making beautiful temples, and he trusted that a constructive dynamic would result from the encounter. Huram, the master craftsman that King Hiram selected to oversee much of the artistic work of the Temple with great attention to detail and beauty, represents in his personal cultural duality a fruitful blending of Israelite and Phoenician societies in such a way that contributed to the growth and success of Israelite religion. (Relating back to chapter 4, Huram is also another biblical example of a positive benefit to the Jewish people resulting from an intermarriage.)

The rabbis who developed midrash chose to paint King Hiram in a negative light, perhaps reflecting their own discomfort with the Bible's apparent positivity towards this polytheistic key supporter of the building of the First Temple. But if we take the Bible on its own terms, we have to reckon with the mythic meaning it may want to present us in its account of the building of the First Temple. The symbolism of the story intends to teach us something larger than just an historical account. The involvement of King Hiram, of Huram the master artist, and of the Phoenician craftsmen point to a profound biblical endorsement of embracing creative openness as a vital element in building up and beautifying the worship of the God of Israel.

In truth, Jethro's legal system and King Hiram's assistance with the First Temple are two examples of a larger reality that much of Israelite religion was influenced by or, in some cases, even derived from the prac-

---

8. The Bible scholar Jon D. Levenson notes that the first Temple "was executed by Phoenician craftsmen (1 Kgs 7:13–14) and [its] design and decoration, as described by the Bible, are familiar to archaeologists from the excavation of the temples of other peoples in the area." Levenson, *Sinai and Zion*, 120.

tices and beliefs of neighbors. And yet, ancient Israel's creative openness did not diminish its authentic uniqueness. The biblical scholar Jon D. Levenson puts it like this:

> [Ancient Israel's] laws resemble Mesopotamian law; her Temple is typically Canaanite; even her monotheism . . . is composed of elements attested outside herself, all of them older than she. It could, of course, be argued that the overall configuration of these elements is unique to Israel, that the bricks may be found elsewhere, but the building is distinctive. This is true. It is, however, also true of the other cultures [of the ancient world]. There never was another Egypt, another Sumer, another Babylonia, another Canaan, another Greece, another Rome. Every complex culture is, in its totality, unique.[9]

Following the biblical era, we find many more examples of Judaism continuing to adapt creatively and grow in depth and meaning through its willingness to stay open to ideas, beliefs, and practices from surrounding civilizations. This is not to say that Judaism has been a hollow open vessel—far from it. Briggs and Peat make clear that a creative open system has a distinct and individual identity, including a unique energy pattern that the system generates and a boundary that distinguishes between itself and the outside world. But a system is not a solid thing like a boulder or a ball on a pool table. Rather, a human system, such as a religious tradition, is a living entity, and in order to stay healthy its boundary needs to be permeable so that it can live in an interconnected and interpenetrating relationship with the world around it. On the biological level this happens through breathing, eating, and taking in sunlight. A living organism is not less authentically itself because it takes in food and air from the environment around it. Similarly, a culture or religion is not less true to itself when it functions as a creative open system. We need to let go of purely mechanistic imagery to describe human systems like nations and religions, and instead adopt a more flowing and fluid sense of how groups truly function.

Two more examples of Jewish creative adaptations that developed after the biblical era can drive this point home. They involve two elements of Jewish tradition that are as quintessentially Jewish as anything one could imagine—the Passover *seder* and the *dreidel* of Hanukkah—both of

9. Ibid., 10.

which came into Judaism in large measure as borrowings from neighboring cultures.

Let's start with the seder. The ancient Greeks had a traditional meal called a symposium, in which the hosts would invite people to come to their home to spend an evening discussing a philosophical topic while dining and drinking. Invitations announced the topic of discussion and the number of cups of wine to be served. The early rabbis borrowed the Greek symposium as the model for the Passover seder. The topic for the evening's discourse: the liberation from slavery under Pharaoh. Total cups of wine: four. Even the dessert at the seder retains its Greek name: *afikomen.*

The early rabbis who did this knew exactly what they were doing, and we have no evidence that it troubled them at all. During the biblical era—before the rabbis' time—there had been a very different method of celebrating Passover. The ancient Israelites would make a pilgrimage to the Temple in Jerusalem and offer specific sacrifices to God. But after the Romans destroyed the Temple and exiled the Jews from the Land of Israel in 70 CE, the way that Passover was celebrated needed to be reconstructed if it was to survive as a festival at all. Through creative openness, the ancient rabbis borrowed a Greek structure and adapted it, filling it with Jewish content and opening up new possibilities for what Jews would focus on and emphasize in their Passover celebrations. The adaptation was a tremendous success. What could be more Jewish than a Passover seder?

Similarly, in medieval Germany, there was a gambling game among the majority Christian population that involved a pot of coins and the spinning of a four-sided top bearing the letters "n," "g," "h," and "s." The letters stood for German words that told the player how much of the money in the pot she would win, or how much she would have to add to the pot from her own money. N was for *nichts* (nothing), G for *ganz* (all, meaning winning all the money in the pot), H for *halb* (half), and S for *stell* (put something in). Jews absorbed the dreidel game into Hanukkah, substituting Hebrew letters for German: *nun* replaced "n," *gimmel* replaced "g," *hey* replaced "h," and *shin* replaced "s." The Jewish version of dreidel retained the German system of determining what the player would do after each spin (*gimmel* means you win everything in the pot, for instance). Even though Jews absorbed this game from their medieval Christian neighbors, what could be more Jewish than spinning the dreidel during Hanukkah?

The seder and the dreidel are not aberrations. Integrating outside elements is one of the main ways that Judaism has survived and thrived as a religion and as a civilization for so long. Systems theorists would argue that this is one of the key ways that groups stay healthy, relevant, alive.

Furthermore, after a group borrows something and incorporates it, the evolutionary activity doesn't necessarily stop there. For instance, coming back to the story of the dreidel, when medieval German Jews absorbed it into their Hanukkah celebrations, they added a new layer of meaning to the letters on the dreidel by treating the four Hebrew letters as an acronym referring to the great miracle of the Hanukkah story. The four Hebrew letters stand for a four-word sentence in Hebrew, n*es* g*adol* h*ayah* sh*am*, which means, "a great miracle happened there." Since the game was being played by Jews in central Europe, the sentence made geographical sense, since the miracle had taken place in Jerusalem.

Centuries later, with the rebirth of Jewish sovereignty in the modern State of Israel, Jews changed the Hebrew letters on the dreidel to bring the dreidel up to date with current events. Dreidels in Israel have replaced the fourth Hebrew letter in the sequence, *shin,* with the letter *pay*. In this case, *pay* stands for the Hebrew word *poh*, which means "here," and changes the sentence made by all four of the words to read "a great miracle happened *here.*"

There are so many important examples of Jewish borrowing from other societies that I could cite, but I'll limit myself to just a few more. Let's consider again the early rabbis who rose to prominence as the re-organizers of Judaism following the Roman destruction of the Temple in 70 CE. Their relationship with the dominant culture of their area—Greco-Roman culture—was complicated. The rabbis who gave us the great literature of interpretation of the Hebrew Bible—midrash and Talmud—warned against Greek philosophical and religious ideas while simultaneously making use of them. Despite their condemnation of Greek and Roman polytheism and political imperialism, some of the key terms and concepts they used in midrash and Talmud came from Greek, not Hebrew. For example, Greek gave the rabbis the term *Sanhedrin*, the name of the great court of law during the late Second Temple period, as well as the word *apikorus*, meaning a Jew whose religious beliefs and opinions constituted apostasy. They simply spelled the Greek loan words phonetically in Hebrew and integrated the concepts into their evolving religious development of rabbinic Judaism. There are many similar examples.

Jumping ahead in time to the Middle Ages, the great Jewish philosopher Maimonides (1135—1204 CE) studied Neo-Platonic philosophy and science as it had been preserved and developed in Arabic by Islamic scholars like the influential philosopher Abu Nasr al-Farabi. Maimonides' great work of theology and philosophy, *The Guide for the Perplexed*, is written in Arabic and parallels treatises written by Muslim philosophers of his era. Maimonides claimed that the Torah and the philosophy of his time were completely in agreement, and that the correct interpretation of the Torah was one that understood the Torah's teachings as harmonious with the Hellenistic philosophical ideas that were widely accepted among the intelligentsia of his era. For example, since the God of Aristotle was a radiating energy force without a body, Maimonides argued that wherever the Hebrew Bible describes God in anthropomorphic terms, the text is not meant to be taken literally. His ideas were not universally appreciated by his rabbinic peers, some of whom even burned the *Guide* in public.

Nevertheless, Maimonides and other medieval Jewish philosophers forever changed the shape of Jewish religious thought by acting on the premise that two different bodies of knowledge—religious tradition and the philosophy/science of the times—were both valid sources of ultimate truth, and that the best way to get at the truth was to be found through creating a dynamic, mutually informing, and mutually correcting study of the two. The contemporary scholar Rabbi David Hartman describes Maimonides' project of integration as follows, using the metaphoric language of Jerusalem and Athens to refer to Judaism and Greek philosophy, respectively:

> Which city does Maimonides inhabit—Athens or Jerusalem? Perhaps he inhabits neither city—not if they are understood as two polarized frameworks of theoretical and practical virtue. A new, yet old, Jerusalem may emerge once Athens enters into history. The concept of nature and the contemplative ideal inspired by a God who is revealed through the ordered laws of nature may grow in Jerusalem without destroying the city's unique quality. Athens may provide a wider understanding of what the Sinai-moment implicitly demanded. Once the outgrowths of Athens have taken root in the soil of Jerusalem both cities may not need to remain opposing spiritual poles. A new, spiritual synthesis with different

categories may emerge. Man may remain fully within the way of Jerusalem and yet deeply appreciate and appropriate the way of Athens.[10]

The elite Jewish thought of the medieval period treated Judaism as a creative open system, in dialogue with the most sophisticated and researched ideas of the times.

As a final example, let's look briefly at the Jewish mystical field known as kabbalah. The central text of kabbalah is the Zohar, a collection of esoteric and mystical midrashic homilies on the Hebrew Bible that were disseminated in Spain in the thirteenth century by the Jewish mystic Moses de Leon. Kabbalah is brilliant, playful, insightful and engrossing, and it represents a tremendous contribution to the world's great mystical traditions. Its literature fuses midrash—the rabbis' brand of creative running interpretation of the verses of the Hebrew Bible—with a specific set of spiritual and cosmological ideas that come in large part from Neo-Platonic philosophical claims about the inner nature and activity of God. Once again, Greek civilization has left its imprint on something quintessentially Jewish—kabbalah.

Many centuries before Moses de Leon began sharing his manuscripts with fellow Jewish mystics in medieval Spain, Neo-Platonic philosophy offered a description of God that became enormously appealing to mystics of many different religious traditions, including Judaism. Neo-Platonism posits that God is an unknowable Being that radiates Divine energy outward. This energy overflows God's innermost being and forms a kind of concentric sphere around God's innermost being.

The energy in this first sphere removed from the Divine Center is a little bit less pure than the energy at the Source. The first sphere's energy also spills out in all directions and forms a second sphere around the first one, and this process repeats until there are many concentric spheres of energy going farther and farther out from the radiating Source at the center that started it all. The farther one gets from the Divine Source, the less pure and refined the Divine energy.

The Divine energy at the outer spheres takes physical matter—which in this philosophical system is considered coarse and devoid of the Divine energy—and forms it into planets, trees, rocks, oceans, and us. All earthly created matter, including human life, exists in the farthest sphere from the

10. Hartman, *Maimonides*, 7.

Center. The Divine energy that radiates from the Center flows all the way out to the farthest sphere, and it also flows back towards its brilliant and unknowable Source. In fact, the Divine energy in the outer spheres yearns to return to its Source. Human life is very coarse and corrupted due to its cosmic distance from the Center and due to its material nature. But there is some of the Divine energy within us, and through righteous living and proper meditation on the Divine energy and the spheres, we can hope to nurture the Divine energy within us and maximize its chances of reuniting with the Source when we die. By doing so, we can attain immortality through communion with the Divine.

What I have just described is one of the most influential Greek ideas ever to have been shared with humankind. It is also a philosophical and theological underpinning of kabbalah without which there would be no kabbalah as we know it. Accepting this truth about the Hellenistic contribution to Jewish mysticism doesn't diminish the Jewishness of kabbalah. That would only be the case if one insisted that cultures and religions are only authentic if they develop themselves in isolation from others. But as I hope this chapter has shown, that's not how it really works. Just as even the most original musician or painter builds on themes and traditions that they study and appreciate, innovating by combining those elements in novel ways and perhaps adding something new from themselves, so too it is with nations and religions.

Without Woody Guthrie there would be no Bob Dylan as we know his work, and yet there's nothing inauthentic, nothing *un-Dylan-ish* about Dylan's music because of this fact. The originality of his music and the *Dylan-ness* of his music derive from the new ways he worked with the materials that influenced him, and from the unique signature that only he could provide in combining things he learned from others with new insights that came from his musical mind. Likewise, kabbalah is an authentically Jewish, original system of mysticism. Its originality and creativity stem from the way it worked with some non-Jewish, preexisting materials and combined them with preexisting Jewish materials as well as its own new ideas.

Some people in the Jewish community would object to this assertion, insisting on the historical accuracy of kabbalah's mythic account of its own origins. This mythic claim is that the Zohar contains the miraculously recovered ancient transmission of rabbis who lived one thousand or so years before Moses de Leon, and that Aristotle's and Plato's ideas about God don't fit into the picture. What I find worrisome about this kind of insistence on such a "hermetically sealed" account of kabbalah (or other aspects of Judaism) is that it chooses to deny the truth of how human systems like religions stay healthy and evolve. This leads towards treating Judaism in the present day as a closed, limit-cycle system. There's nothing to fear from acknowledging that Judaism has evolved as a creative open system. But there is something to fear from denying this truth in the name of embracing a belief in a "pure and uncontaminated" Judaism that developed apart from the "more profane" world of the non-Jews. In recent years such attitudes have grown in parts of the Jewish community that have embraced new forms of fundamentalism. This is unfortunate, because a life-affirming, relevant, and healthy Judaism can't survive and thrive into the future as a closed system, hunkering down behind imper-meable fortifications and regarding the entire outside world with suspi-cion. Similarly, Christianity and Islam suffer and become unhealthy when they manifest as closed, rigid, limit-cycle systems.

***

Some final thoughts on this topic: many scholars of Judaism write about how one of the keys to Judaism's longevity has been its ability to adapt to change while still retaining a vibrant sense of its own authenticity. Creative openness has indeed been one of the core elements of Judaism's survival and success, but it hasn't happened without controversy or internal strug-gle. Many times during the history of the Jews part of the community has resisted the proposed adaptations to new circumstances.

When the early rabbis, in the decades and first centuries following the Roman destruction of Jerusalem, sought to assert themselves as the new religious authorities of Judaism, it wasn't easy for them. They were claiming to be the proper religious authorities for a religion that had until that time been led by priests, not rabbis, and that, had centered around a Temple that no longer stood. While they had earned the allegiance of parts of the Jewish community in the centuries just prior to the Roman exile, in the post-destruction period they still had to work hard to win over large parts of the Jewish community.

The early rabbis were making the case for massive change to the religion in response to the Roman decimation of the Jewish homeland and the exiling of the Jews to various parts of the empire. They sought to normalize new traditions, and they used different definitions than the priests had used for determining who could become a religious authority. Many Jews rejected their claim to legitimacy, and other groups of Jewish leaders competed with the rabbis for the mantle of authenticity in those early post-destruction years. A major Jewish religious movement that rejected the rabbis and their writings—Karaism—went on to be a potent Jewish counter-force to rabbinic Judaism for over 1,000 years.

Similarly, in the 1700s, many Jews in Eastern and Central Europe embraced an innovative pietistic approach to Jewish life that came to be known as *Hasidism*. The Hasidic rabbis who led this movement faced tremendous resistance from many of their colleagues, who branded them with all kinds of unkind names and denigrated their teachings. Yet eventually hasidism found acceptance and went on to influence mainstream Judaism across the board.

In every era, including today, it seems that Jews have been divided about what sorts of changes to embrace, and which ideas from the outside world to allow through Judaism's permeable membrane so that these ideas can influence the ongoing evolution of Judaism. There are always some who will react to any outside influence, novelty, or adaptation with the impulse to build a solid wall and warn that the "purity of the tradition" is about to be irreversibly polluted. Again, we see parallel conflicts playing out within Christianity and Islam.

What Moses teaches us in his interaction with Jethro in Exodus 18 is that even from its earliest beginnings, Judaism was never a hermetically sealed object, developing apart from the rest of the peoples of the world. Even in its origins, Israelite religion drew on many elements of surrounding religions and cultures. In Exodus 18 Moses treated the religion he was helping to found as a living, complex culture, a creative open system interested in seeking higher truth wherever that truth might be found. When the Priest of Midian was the source of a piece of that truth, Moses didn't hesitate to incorporate it. Moses teaches us here that religions and nations are best able to grow and stay healthy when they are open to influences and ideas from outside themselves. From this we learn that one mark of a religion or a nation's health or sickness is the degree to which it seeks to cut itself off from all others, branding them as impure and polluting, versus the degree to which it has the trust and self-confidence to borrow and lend ideas, beliefs, and ways of doing things.

6

Moses and God

Panim-El-Panim, Ehyeh-Asher-Ehyeh

"It is as though God beckons with one hand and repels with the other."
—Jon D. Levenson, *Sinai and Zion*[1]

"And there never arose again in Israel a prophet like Moses,
whom the Eternal knew face to face."
—Deut 34:10[2]

One of the most remarkable chapters in the Torah is Exodus 33. It's a wonderful case of the Torah's deliberate presentation of paradox, asking us to hold, at the same time, two very different understandings of how human beings experience God. Exodus 33 takes place right after the Hebrews are punished for the sin of the golden calf, and just before Moses is instructed by God to ascend Mount Sinai a second time in order to receive a replacement set of the stone tablets of the Law, since he had smashed the first set in anger when he saw the people worshiping the

1. Levenson, *Sinai and Zion*, 15.
2. Deut 34:10. Translation mine.

golden calf. In reading the following group of verses from Exodus 33, please note that there are two story episodes in succession, the first one comprised of verses 7–11, and the second of verses 12–23.

Story Episode One:

Now Moses used to take a tent and pitch it outside the camp some distance away, calling it the "tent of meeting." Anyone inquiring of the Eternal would go to the tent of meeting outside the camp. And whenever Moses went out to the tent, all the people rose and stood at the entrances to their tents, watching Moses until he entered the tent. As Moses went into the tent, the pillar of cloud would come down and stay at the entrance, while the Eternal spoke with Moses. Whenever the people saw the pillar of cloud standing at the entrance to the tent, they all stood and worshiped, each at the entrance to their tent. *The Eternal would speak to Moses face to face, as one speaks to a friend.* Then Moses would return to the camp, but his young aide Joshua son of Nun did not leave the tent.[3]

Story Episode Two:

Moses said to the Eternal, "You have been telling me, 'Lead these people,' but you have not let me know whom you will send with me. You have said, 'I know you by name and you have found favor with me.' If you are pleased with me, teach me your ways so I may know you and continue to find favor with you. Remember that this nation is your people."

The Eternal replied, "My Presence will go with you, and I will give you rest."

Then Moses said to him, "If your Presence does not go with us, do not send us up from here. How will anyone know that you are pleased with me and with your people unless you go with us? What else will distinguish me and your people from all the other people on the face of the earth?"

And the Eternal said to Moses, "I will do the very thing you have asked, because I am pleased with you and I know you by name."

Then Moses said, "Now show me your glory."

And the Eternal said, "I will cause all my goodness to pass in front of you, and I will proclaim my name, the Eternal, in your presence. I will have mercy on whom I will have mercy, and I will

3. Exod 33:7–11, *NIV* (adapted). Italics mine.

have compassion on whom I will have compassion. But," God said, *"you cannot see my face, for no human may see me and live."*

Then the Eternal said, "There is a place near me where you may stand on a rock. When my glory passes by, I will put you in a cleft in the rock and cover you with my hand until I have passed by. Then I will remove my hand and you will see my back; *but my face must not be seen."*[4]

In these verses we find the Torah telling us first that God and Moses spoke "face to face, as one speaks to a friend," and then only moments later in the narrative God tells Moses, "you cannot see my face, for no human may see me and live." These two statements are only nine verses apart! The key Hebrew word in these passages is the word *panim* and close variations upon it. *Panim* means "face." *Panim* and related words also connote intimacy, not only because face-to-face conversation is inherently intimate, but because in Hebrew this word also means "inner" or "internal." In verse 11, God speaks to Moses *panim-el-panim*, face to face. In verse 20, God tells Moses that no one can see *panai*—"My face"—and survive the experience. The chapter concludes with God telling Moses that *panai* won't be seen.

In the first episode (vv. 7–11) we learn about Moses' conversations with God in the Tent of Meeting, and the Torah teaches us that there was an informal nature to the face-to-face interactions between the two of them. They spoke like friends, or neighbors, as other translations have it. This is a stunning statement considering the awesome power and miraculous wonders of this God, and the human frailty of any person—even someone as exemplary as Moses. God and Moses shot the breeze together in the tent!

The second episode (vv. 12–23) reads almost like a text that is totally unaware of the first episode's existence. Moses pleads for God not to require that he take the Hebrews on the journey through the wilderness without God's accompanying the people, and God offers a concession. God's presence will travel with them. Then, as if this episode seeks to stress how different it is from the one that preceded it, Moses pleads that God show him God's glory (= face? truest nature?), but God explains that this is something that just can't be done, adding: "My face must not be seen."

4. Exod 33:12–23, *NIV* (adapted). Italics mine.

So, what are these two contradictory episodes doing side by side (or, face to face, if you'll forgive the pun)? Did the Torah mean to cause us to get to the last words of Exodus 33—God telling Moses, "My face must not be seen"—and ask out loud, "Wait a minute! What happened to the face-to-face conversations you two were just having in the Tent? Why is Moses still alive if he saw God's face in verses 7–11? And which One are You, God—the Deity a person can talk to like a best buddy, or the Awesome One whose being is so unknowable and mind-blowing that to glimpse Its true essence would fry us in an instant?"

What are the Torah and Moses trying to teach us in these curiously consecutive episodes? It can't be accidental that these contradictory declarations about how humans can or can't encounter God are placed one right after the other in the Torah. For people who profess a traditional belief about the origin of the Torah, of course, there are no accidents in the placement of any of the words, because they believe that God authored the entire text and meant for us to puzzle over its apparent contradictions and its masterful paradoxes. For those of us, including liberal rabbis like me, who assume that the Torah is made up of different source materials that were, over much time, edited together to form the book as a whole, the fact remains that verses 7–11 and verses 12–23 appear side by side on purpose. The final editors of the Torah (the "redactors," in the terminology of biblical scholarship) put these two accounts about the nature of God's and Moses' interactions side by side knowing that people would see the contradiction and ask some version of the question, "Hey, what's going on here?"

So what *is* the Torah trying to teach? Perhaps looking elsewhere in the Torah we can find some clues. The seventeen verses we've been considering aren't the only place that the Torah presents the encounter between human and Deity as either surprisingly informal and intimate, on the one hand, or distant, inscrutable, and awe-inspiring, on the other. In Genesis 18, God arrives at Abraham and Sarah's tent in the form of an unexpected guest and receives their gracious hospitality. In that scene, Abraham speaks with God like a person, face to face (though in this instance the Torah doesn't employ those specific words). In contrast, when Moses is first called by God at the burning bush, he encounters God only as a disembodied voice in the midst of the flames. Seeking a more intimate knowledge of God, Moses asks God to tell him God's name. But God only replies cryptically, *ehyeh-asher-ehyeh*, "I will be that I will be," or, as some have translated it, "I am that I am." As Judy Klitsner writes regarding the Torah, "At times [God] is transcendent and infallible . . . Yet in other instances, God is described in . . . shockingly human terms."[5]

The Torah also presents us with images of God's presence that are terrifying and overwhelming in some cases, yet subtle and small in others. Just before the giving of the Ten Commandments, Exodus 19 describes God's presence this way (majestically rendered in the 1917 Jewish Publication Society translation): "there were thunders and lightnings and a thick cloud upon the mount, and the voice of a horn exceeding loud; and all the people that were in the camp trembled. And Moses brought forth the people out of the camp to meet God; and they stood at the nether part of the mount. Now Mount Sinai was altogether on smoke, because the Eternal descended upon it in fire; and the smoke thereof ascended as the smoke of a furnace, and the whole mount quaked greatly."[6]

Contrast the fireworks of the revelation at Mount Sinai with the scene that took place earlier at that same mountain, when Moses first noticed God's presence in the form of a small desert bush that had caught on fire and yet, somehow, was not consumed by the fire. Many rabbis have commented on how understated this Divine self-presentation was, noting that in a desert climate a burning scrub brush would not be terribly unusual. Moses had to stop and take the time to watch the bush carefully in order to see that the fire was not consuming it. This is the kind of miracle that doesn't even appear to be a miracle to the average onlooker. Elaborating on this point centuries later, the rabbis gave us the following story in midrash: "A certain gentile once asked Rabbi Joshua ben Korcha: 'Why did the Holy One, blessed be He, see fit to speak with Moses from a burning bush?' [Rabbi Joshua] said to him: 'Had it been from a burning carob tree, or from a burning sycamore, you would have asked me the same thing. But to send you out empty-handed is impossible; why out of a burning bush? To teach you that there is no place void of the Shechinah [the Divine Presence], not even a bush.'"[7]

---

5. Klitsner, *Subversive Sequels in the Bible*, xxiii–xxv.

6. Exod 19:16–18, *OJPS* (adapted).

7. Navon, *Genesis and Jewish Thought*, 9. The author has quoted a midrash from *Shemot Rabbah* 2.

The German Bible scholar Elias Auerbach, noticed that the Hebrew word for the bush where God first spoke to Moses is *sneh*, and the Hebrew name of the mountain where later Moses experiences God in volcanic thundering and smoldering smoke is the linguistically similar *sinai*.[8] The two words are closely linked, and together present a microcosm of one of the great dualisms that the Torah offers us about the different ways we may experience God. The American Bible scholar Jon D. Levenson describes the link between *sneh* and *sinai* like this:

> In the encounter of Moses and the burning bush, two of YHWH's emblems—tree and fire—clash, and neither overpowers the other. The two will appear again in tandem in the [menorah], the Tabernacle candelabrum which is actually a stylized tree, complete with "branches," "almond shaped cups," "calyxes," and "petals" (Exod 25:31–39). This arborescent lampstand appears not only in the Tabernacle which served as Israel's central sanctuary in the period of wandering in the wilderness, but also in the Temple that was to be built by Solomon [during the period of the monarchy] . . . The Temple at Jerusalem was lit by the fires of the burning tree.[9]

The Torah means for us to understand that the encounter between God and human can be spectacular or private, immanent or transcendent, intimate or forbidding. For Levenson, the ancient Temple's ritual lampstand, whose flame was kept lit throughout each night, was a symbol of both facets of the encounter with God. The menorah combined the divine fire upon Mount Sinai with the simple small tree (or bush) of Moses' private, first direct encounter with God.

The presenting of these two images—a mountain in fiery thunder and a small tree—in the paradoxical combination of a burning bush that is not consumed relates a message to us about the nature of God's being. It's as if God is trying to say, "You can know me intimately (*panim-el-panim* / face to face) *and* I am utterly unknowable (*ehyeh-asher-ehyeh* / I will be what I will be). I am both Friend and Creator of the Universe." Rabbi Sybil Sheridan puts it this way, "Moses has a much closer relationship to God than anyone ever had, but it's still an elusive one. We understand through Moses that although we can get very, very close, God remains always beyond us. We can never define God."[10]

8. Auerbach, *Moses*, 29.

9. Levenson, *Sinai and Zion*, 20–21.

10. Sheridan, "Moses."

***

We find another biblical story that presents this dance with the Divine—now you know me up close, now you can't possibly know my inner Being—in the Genesis account of Jacob wrestling with God:

> So Jacob was left alone, and a man wrestled with him till daybreak. When the man saw that he could not overpower him, he touched the socket of Jacob's hip so that his hip was wrenched as he wrestled with the man. Then the man said, "Let me go, for it is daybreak."
>
> But Jacob replied, "I will not let you go unless you bless me."
>
> The man asked him, "What is your name?"
>
> "Jacob," he answered.
>
> Then the man said, "Your name will no longer be Jacob, but Israel, because you have struggled with God and with men and have overcome."
>
> Jacob said, "Please tell me your name."
>
> But he replied, "Why do you ask my name?"
>
> Then he blessed him there. So Jacob called the place *Peni-El*, saying, "It is because I saw God face to face, and yet my life was spared."[11]

This story ends with Jacob, now called Israel, declaring that he has seen God in the same way Moses has: *panim-el-panim*, face to face. Jacob names the place *Peni-El*, which means, "Face of God." And yet, just as Moses experiences personal intimacy with God as well as unapproachable barriers to truly knowing God, likewise Jacob has an intensely intimate and physical experience with God, and yet his effort to learn God's name is met with evasion. It's as if God wants to say, "You can wrestle Me, feel My sweat against yours, even pin My very body down on the ground and have victory over Me"—look at the text, it's there!"—and yet you cannot know my Name. Why do you even ask?"

***

For the ancient rabbis who gave us midrash and the Talmud, apparent contradictions in Torah were cause for interpretive maneuvers to reconcile the contradictions and reaffirm their theological belief in God as the

---

11. Gen 32:25–31 in Jewish editions of the Bible, vv. 24–30 in Christian editions. *NIV* (adapted). Italics mine.

sole author of the Torah. Sometimes this approach led to creative religious insights that are among the jewels of Judaism. Other times rabbinic interpretive maneuvers paved over the intentional presentation of contradiction in the Torah. The Bible sometimes presents these contradictions in the form of paradox, or in what the Bible scholar Robert Alter calls "composite artistry."[12]

In his classic book, *The Art of Biblical Narrative*, Alter writes about the final editors of the Torah—the redactors—and their artistic method of intentionally crafting a literary composite work from various source materials. The redactors' way of weaving together texts from different sources and adding in some new material of their own expressed artistic and religious meaning in a way that was familiar and comfortable to them and their contemporary audiences. The redactors' final product arose from the "editing and splicing and artful montage of antecedent literary materials,"[13] mixed in with some writing of their own. The redactors gave us a Torah that is "a loom work of interwoven sources."[14]

Alter believes that the redactors were more than mere editors (or clumsy editors, as some academics have asserted over the years). No, the redactors were artists in their own right, skillfully selecting the elements they worked with and patterning them according to artistic intentions that made sense in their own literary times. Sometimes they chose to include successive passages that presented theological contradictions like the one we've been examining. Sometimes they purposefully chose to include multiple accounts of the same story. In many cases they presented us with two accounts of the same events that include glaring inconsistencies. In fact, when we look at the first two chapters of Genesis, we see that that is how the redactors chose to begin the entire Torah.

Many Bible scholars have discussed how Genesis opens with two accounts of the creation of the universe that contradict each other in several major ways. For example, in the first account (Gen 1:1—2:3), all the animals are created before the first human, but in the second account (Gen 2:4—3:24) Adam is created before the animals. And in the first account, God creates the first human simultaneously male and female, whereas in the second account Adam, the male, is created first, and only after he

12. Alter, *The Art of Biblical Narrative*. "Composite Artistry" is the title of chapter 7.

13. Ibid., 140.

14. Visotzky, *Reading the Book*, 31.

becomes lonely does God cast a deep sleep on him and remove one of his ribs to create Eve. And there are other contradictions as well.

Why would the redactors of the Torah choose to violate narrative consistency in such an obvious way right from the beginning? Alter explains that it is we, the heirs to Western modern literary conventions, who expect a certain kind of narrative and logical consistency from our storytelling, but that the literary and storytelling conventions for the ancient Israelites were different.[15]

In discussing the two contradictory accounts of creation, he writes, "[the redactors of the Torah] chose to combine these two versions of creation precisely because [they] understood that [their] subject was essentially contradictory, essentially resistant to consistent linear formulation, and . . . this was [their] way of giving it the most adequate literary expression."[16] Alter describes this "composite artistry" further with this analogy:

> The decision to place in sequence two ostensibly contradictory accounts of the same event is an approximate narrative equivalent to the technique of post-Cubist painting which gives us, for example, juxtaposed or superimposed, a profile and a frontal perspective of the same face. The ordinary eye could never see these two at once, but it is the painter's prerogative to represent them as a simultaneous perception within the visual frame of his painting, whether merely to explore the formal relations of the two views or to provide an encompassing representation of his subject. Analogously, the Hebrew writer takes advantage of the composite nature of his art to give us a tension of views that will govern most of the biblical stories . . .[17]

Judy Klitsner argues that the Hebrew Bible deliberately presents certain stories followed by other complementary or contradictory stories in order to reconsider and sometimes even subvert the claims, beliefs, and assumptions of the first story. In the introduction to her book *Subversive Sequels in the Bible: How Biblical Stories Mine and Undermine Each Other*, she writes:

15. Alter, *The Art of Biblical Narrative*; see especially chapter 7, "Composite Artistry."
16. Ibid., 145.
17. Ibid., 146.

> As if aware of its own problematics, the Bible contains a lively inter-
> action between its passages that allows for a widening of perspec-
> tive and a sense of dynamic development throughout the canon . . .
> [I]f certain gnawing theological or philosophical questions remain
> after studying one narrative, a later passage may revisit those ques-
> tions, subjecting them to a complex process of inquiry, revision,
> and examination of alternative possibilities. I call these reworkings
> "subversive sequels." Like all sequels, they continue and complete
> earlier stories. But they do so in ways that often undermine the
> very assumptions upon which the earlier stories were built as well
> as the conclusions these stories have reached.[18]

I think Alter and Klitsner have uncovered some of the spirit in which
the Torah's redactors chose to present us with Exodus 33's two conflicting
claims about whether or not Moses saw God's face. *Exodus 33's consecutive episodes are commenting on the contradictory and logic-defying nature
of the intense human-Divine encounter.* There are times in our lives when
the encounter with a Higher Power or Ultimate Truth is private, simple,
subtle, informal, intimate, face to face, as it were. There are times when
the encounter is from the distanced vantage point of not being able to
know who or what the Ultimate One is, when we simply are beyond our
mind's capacity to grasp what we're dealing with, when we cannot know
God's name or face, when all God can tell us is what God said to Moses:
ehyeh-asher-ehyeh, "I am that I am."

What Torah teaches us in Exodus 33 and what Moses teaches us in
his two contradictory encounters with God is that when it comes to the
experiences and events in our lives that connect us with higher meaning,
or that cause us to discover Truth, we don't need for all of it to make some
kind of logical sense. So what if it doesn't all make sense? The nature of
some aspects of Reality may be nonlinear, may be of a composite nature,
with contradictory elements sitting alongside each other and creating a
paradoxical tension that may be part of the truth of our own encounters with the Divine in our lives. *Panim-el-panim* and *ehyeh-asher-ehyeh*
are invitations to us to try to stay open to the different ways the Divine
manifests in our lives, and the composite artistry of Torah is an invitation
for us to remember that Western linear and logically consistent storytelling is not the only way to think about the world or experience reality.
We've entered a realm, to quote Alter once more, in which the subject

18. Klitsner, *Subversive Sequels in the Bible,* xvi.

itself is "essentially contradictory, essentially resistant to consistent linear formulation."[19]

The contemporary Christian theologian Val Webb proposes that the contradictory descriptions of God's nature found in religious sacred texts point towards an overarching understanding of God that she terms "Formlessness."[20] She writes, "With no one shape, existence, or description, Formlessness can equally be anything . . . Formlessness also has the potential to take any shape, fill any space, operate free of limits, be imaged in a multitude of ways, and yet not limited to any one."[21] More directly applicable to our study of the contradictory passages in Exodus 33, she adds, "The ability of Formlessness to remain formless or take any form gives rise to contradictions in GOD-talk—known yet unknown, present yet hidden, closer than our breath yet not contained by the highest heavens . . . within us yet transcendent, speaking yet staying silent, and so on."[22]

Another thought: the composite view that Alter describes the Hebrew Bible offering us can serve as a warning to us not to mistake a partial truth for the whole. If we were to take just one of the two episodes that we've been examining in Exodus 33 and never read the other, we could come away with a very satisfying sense that we've just encountered "the truth" at the heart of the question of how people experience the Divine in their lives. If we only read vv. 7–11, then the lesson would be that the truly authentic experience of God's presence is the profoundly intimate encounter, as represented by the image of two people talking face to face. Checking this idea against our own experience, many of us would find that this notion rings true. If we had only read vv. 12–23, on the other hand, we would have found the Torah and Moses testifying to the idea that God is beyond our knowing, our naming, or our seeing. God's "otherness" is so complete and mysterious that we can't hope to know what It actually is. Again, checking this idea against our own experience, many of us would feel that this rings true, and given the stamp of traditional authority that the Bible tends to provide, the possibility of seeing this as the whole truth would be there.

19. Alter, *The Art of Biblical Narrative*, 145.
20. Webb, *Like Catching Water in a Net*, 66.
21. Ibid.
22. Ibid., 67.

By giving us both snapshots, this seventeen-verse passage of the Torah jars us with conflicting accounts of Moses' experiences of God, but more importantly it jars loose from us the temptation to see only one of these accounts as the *whole* truth. Each account appears to be a partial truth, and the fact that together they create a logical impossibility is part of the paradox we're left with. We're also left with the opportunity to learn a kind of intellectual and spiritual humility. The truth that we experience or discover may only be partial. Even things that seem logically impossible according to the truth we've discovered might in fact be part of the larger truth—the *whole* truth. The composite artistry of Torah creates a multivocal text, a text that lets us see more than one perspective on complex, mysterious, or even not fully comprehensible truths.

This aspect of multiple perspectives being part of the nature of Torah wasn't lost on the ancient rabbis. In the midrashic collection known as *Pesikta de Rav Kahana*, one sage taught: "The Holy One appeared to [the Jews at Mount Sinai] as though He were a statue with faces on every side. A thousand people might be looking at the statue, but it would appear to be looking at each one of them."[23] And a different rabbi in the same text similarly stated:

> The Divine Word spoke to each and every person according to his particular capacity. And do not be surprised at this idea. For when manna came down for Israel, each and every person tasted it in keeping with his own capacity—infants in keeping with their capacity; young men in keeping with their capacity; and the elderly in keeping with their capacity . . . Now what was true about the manna—that each and every person tasted it according to his own particular capacity—was equally true about the Divine Word. Each and every person heard it according to his own particular capacity . . . Therefore the Holy One said: "Do not be misled because you hear many voices. Know ye that I am He who is one and the same: I am the Lord thy God."[24]

So Torah presents us with the reality that people encounter partial truths, even in their most profound encounters with God. The midrash above, as well as Exodus 33, warn us not to assume that what we have seen, heard, tasted, or felt is the only possible experience of the Divine.

23. *Pesikta de Rav Kahana* 12:25. Quoted by Holtz in *Torah from JTS*.
24. *Pesikta de Rav Kahana* 12:25. Quoted by Holtz in *Torah from JTS*.

Danah Zohar and Ian Marshall, in their book *The Quantum Society*, describe the partial nature of our encounters with truth by way of analogies from quantum physics. Quantum physics has revealed a subatomic picture of matter and energy that includes multiple possible states of reality coexisting in a suspended state of potential being. Sometimes these various potential states are contradictory, and yet they are equally real, equally part of the observable and measurable science of quantum physics. Zohar and Marshall, who apply the ideas of quantum physics to human society and religion, make the case that ultimate truth is also quantum in nature. They call this "quantum reality."

Their thoughts on the insights that "quantum reality" offers on the nature of truth echo the multifaceted picture of truth that the composite artistry of the Torah gives us through its presentation of different and contradictory partial truths side by side. They write, "Quantum reality shows us that there can be many points of view, or many faces of truth, some even mutually contradictory, and yet all equally real in the potential sense that all of the quantum realm has existence."[25] Zohar and Marshall elaborate further, explaining how their understanding of the truth having many faces is not a simple slide into a philosophy of relativism:

> it is not true that "truth" is only our relative point of view, and that one "truth" is as good as any other. There are criteria. There is an underlying reality there...We are in dialogue with *something*. It is just that that something has many faces, many potentialities, and that the more of those faces we can know the closer we will come to being in touch with the larger underlying reality... [T]he multifaceted nature of quantum reality... call[s] upon us to accept the partial nature of the truths to which we can have access... [T]hese partial truths are but the obtainable faces of a deeper, underlying, though ultimately inexpressible, truth . . . This is a maturity that allows me to be a committed Christian or a committed Jew, a committed advocate of my own vision of the good or the true or the beautiful, *while at the same time* allowing me to acknowledge that my way is only one possible way.[26]

Torah, midrash, and contemporary philosophers like Zohar and Marshall all present us with guidance to approach the human experience

25. Zohar and Marshall, *The Quantum Society*, 153.
26. Ibid., 154–55. Italics are the authors.'

of truth—or the human encounter with God—as an opportunity to recognize the partial nature of the moments of truth we discover.

***

Let's return to Moses' experience of seeing God's face. What might that kind of experience be like for us? When do we see God's face? Two twentieth-century Jewish philosophers, Germany's Martin Buber and France's Emmanuel Levinas, taught on this question. Buber taught that God is found in the genuine interactions between a person and another, between "I and Thou." When we are truly receptive and open to receiving the Other as a subject and not an object, and we let our hearts act with empathy in response, then we experience God in relationship. Levinas took this line of thought a step further in terms of the importance of the face-to-face encounter. For Levinas, when we encounter another person, the very moment we meet him or her we become morally responsible for his or her well-being. Specifically, the experience of seeing the Other's *face* commands us to be responsible for that person's welfare. His use of the language of command is striking, as in a Jewish context the only "commander" one can find is God; so in a sense, for Levinas, each encounter we have with another person is an encounter with God, and each face we see is the face of God.

In Genesis, the Hebrew phrase "the face of God" occurs in a story that relates directly to Buber's and Levinas' thoughts.[27] The scene is twenty years after Jacob had fled his parents' home in the land of Canaan because his twin brother, Esau, was so full of rage at him that he hoped to kill Jacob. Esau's anger became murderous because, after having already been humiliated and outwitted by Jacob in the past, Jacob had tricked him out of their father's final blessing intended for Esau as firstborn. Now, two decades later, Jacob is making his return to Canaan, and he has been given word that Esau has set out upon the road to meet him, with a retinue of four hundred men. The situation is tense when the estranged brothers finally see each other for the first time. Here is what happened: "[Jacob] went on ahead and bowed down to the ground seven times as he ap-

27. Gen 33.

proached his brother. But Esau ran to meet Jacob and embraced him; he threw his arms around his neck and kissed him. And they wept."[28]

A few moments later Esau asks Jacob why he had received so many gifts from Jacob in the days leading up to their meeting on the road. Jacob responds honestly: "To find favor in your eyes, my lord."[29] Esau tells Jacob that he has plenty of material wealth and suggests that Jacob take back the gifts, possibly out of concern that his brother is not so rich. Jacob's response is striking. "'No, please!' said Jacob. 'If I have found favor in your eyes, accept this gift from me. For to see your face is like seeing the face of God, now that you have received me favorably.'"[30]

Interestingly, the last place the Torah mentions Jacob having been before his reconciliation with Esau is the very place where he wrestled with God, the place that Jacob had named *Peni-El*, "face of God." He leaves the site of an encounter with God that made him feel he had seen God face to face, and then has a cathartic reconciliation with his worst enemy. And in that moment of weeping and letting go of the hatred of the past, Jacob again sees God's face—the face of Esau.

28. Gen 33:3–4, *NIV.*
29. Gen 33:8, *NIV.*
30. Gen 33:10, *NIV.*

7

The Law of Moses Can Be
Challenged and Changed

"The demonstration that human beings can influence even God is all over
the Torah. Moshe Rabbenu [Moses our Rabbi] influences God. Avraham
Avinu [Abraham our Father] influences God. [The Holy One, Blessed Be He]
wishes to learn from His conversations with human beings ... That's what
[covenant] is about. The whole engagement is not about God's control but
about God's love; because God engages human beings, says what God thinks,
and they say back, and He goes, 'Oh ...' God says, 'Oh, you know what? That's
right. You know what? Let's do it this way instead.'"

—RABBI STEVE GREENBERG, THE FIRST OPENLY GAY ORTHODOX RABBI[1]

"Rav, Rabbi Hanina, and Rabbi Yohanan taught ... Anyone who can protest to his
or her household and does not—he or she is accountable for the wrongdoings
of his or her household. Likewise, if a person could protest to the people of his
or her city and does not—he or she is accountable for their wrongdoings. If one
could protest to the whole world and does not, he or she is accountable for the
wrongdoings of the whole world."

—BABYLONIAN TALMUD. TRACTATE SHABBAT 54B[2]

1. *Trembling Before G-d*. Directed by Sandi Simcha Dubowsky, 2001.
2. BT 56b. Translation mine.

TOWARDS THE END OF the Israelites' forty years of wandering in the wilderness, the Torah records an episode about the daughters of a man named Tzelophehad. The five women's names are recorded as Mahlah, Noah, Hoglah, Milcah, and Tirtzah.[3] Their father had died without siring any sons, and the Israelite laws of land distribution that God had handed down (Num 26:52–56)[4] did not allow daughters to inherit. The women brought a challenge to the law, arguing that their deceased father's inheritance should pass to them, and not to his closest male relative as the law required, or else their father's name would disappear for all time. Moses had recently taken a census of the Israelites as they prepared for their conquest of Canaan, and soon plans were to be made for how the territory would be divided up: by tribe, by clan, and by household. The five sisters were worried that the land bearing the name of their father's household would be merged into another male relative's allotment. They presented their case in public, before Moses and the High Priest.

It's a fascinating moment in Moses' leadership. The law that he has presented the Israelites—the law of God—has just been challenged, and by a group of women no less (keeping in mind the patriarchal nature of the society at the time). And the challenge has come in public, in front of the community. Dramatically, it's as if all eyes are on Moses, waiting to see how he will react. Will he take their challenge as an unacceptable affront to his (and God's) law? Will he censure these women for even daring to speak?

What Moses and God end up doing has huge implications for how we choose to look at law, whether in a religious or a secular context. First, Moses doesn't act threatened by the appeal, and in fact simply seems stumped. On the one hand, there is the existing law of inheritance, which is clear. On the other hand, the daughters' case seems to have some merit. Moses takes the case directly to God.

God hears the case, considers it, and then rules in favor of the sisters. A new, revised law is proclaimed:

---

3. See Num 27 for the entire episode.

4. Rabbi Silvina Chemen writes that these verses refer to the men who were counted in the census that takes up most of Num 26, as the people who are eligible to receive a land allotment in the Promised Land, and that this law precludes the daughters of any man who died without sons from inheriting his allotment. In Eskenazi and Weiss, *The Torah: A Women's Commentary*, 985–86.

> So Moses brought their case before the Eternal, and the Eternal
> said to him, "What Zelophehad's daughters are saying is right.
> You must certainly give them property as an inheritance among
> their father's relatives and turn their father's inheritance over to
> them. Say to the Israelites, 'If a man dies and leaves no son, turn
> his inheritance over to his daughter. If he has no daughter, give his
> inheritance to his brothers. If he has no brothers, give his inheri-
> tance to his father's brothers. If his father had no brothers, give his
> inheritance to the nearest relative in his clan, that he may possess
> it. This is to be a legal requirement for the Israelites, as the Eternal
> commanded Moses.'"[5]

New Divine law emerges following an appeal from citizens! And not
citizens who occupy positions of privilege, but women—*daughters*—in a
society based on patriarchal households and clans. Here the Torah seems
to be saying that there is no authority—not even Moses or God—who is
above questioning, and a just appeal can lead to a change in the law.

And as if to emphasize this point, the law of inheritance isn't done
being appealed and changed in the Torah. The last chapter of the book of
Numbers, chapter 36, tells the story of a group that brings an appeal over
the new law that was created as a result of the daughters' appeal! Leaders
of the daughters' Israelite tribe appear before Moses and present a problem they see with the new law. Now that the daughters will inherit their
father's land share, if they should go on to marry men who belong to one
of the other eleven Israelite tribes, then their land will be absorbed into
the tribes of their husbands. The daughters' tribe will end up losing some
of its territory as a result.

Once again, Moses brings the appeal before God, and once again
God rules in favor of the challengers. God revises the law of inheritance
again:

> Then at the Eternal's command Moses gave this order to the
> Israelites: ". . . This is what the Eternal commands for Zelophehad's
> daughters: They may marry anyone they please as long as they
> marry within the tribal clan of their father. No inheritance in
> Israel is to pass from tribe to tribe, for every Israelite shall keep
> the tribal land inherited from his forefathers. Every daughter who
> inherits land in any Israelite tribe must marry someone in her fa-
> ther's tribal clan, so that every Israelite will possess the inheritance

5. Num 27:5–11, *NIV* (adapted).

of his fathers. No inheritance may pass from tribe to tribe, for each Israelite tribe is to keep the land it inherits."[6]

Now, in my work in a liberal synagogue with a strongly held value of gender equality, this second revision of the inheritance law tends to diminish some of the excitement that congregants feel after reading the first revision. A text that presents an ancient Israelite example of expanding women's rights takes a turn and concludes with a new restriction on those very women, seriously limiting whom they are allowed to marry.

We have a lot to learn about gender roles in the tribal patriarchy of the Israelites from these two legal appeals, and I don't mean to diminish the importance of that discussion. But if we can set that question aside for a moment, leaving the content of the appeals out and simply looking at the mechanics of how the law is being challenged, reconsidered, and changed, we discover something important about the Law of Moses. It is subject to repeated appeal. It can change.

Instead of the popular image of Moses handing down laws etched in stone—eternal, unchanging, commanding us forever to obey—we have something different here. We have in these texts a living and evolving legal relationship between God and the people. In the context of that relationship, the people can have input that influences God, and that even changes God's thinking. It doesn't matter whether the people are men or women, powerful or weak, self-interested or seeking to benefit others—there is an opportunity provided for questioning and appeal, and there is a Divine Being on the other end of that conversation who is listening and *who can learn from us.* One could even posit a radical theology based on the two passages under consideration—a theology in which God and the people have a covenantal relationship in which both parties coevolve, growing and learning from each other. Judy Klitsner sees exactly such a growing and changing God in her reading of Torah:

> For many [people], the notion of the dynamic nature of humanity may be far more palatable than ascribing an evolutionary nature to God. But the concept of God's development is not new in Jewish tradition . . . modern scholars have found ample evidence of it throughout the Bible's pages. By viewing God as a literary character and monitoring His development between one biblical story and the next, we are privy to one of the central and most consistent

6. Num 36:5–9, *NIV* (adapted).

messages of the [Hebrew Bible] as a whole, namely the ideal of constant movement and growth.[7]

Whatever the theological implications are of these biblical passages, what they offer us is a model of law that resists unthinking obedience. This is a kind of law that is improved by people having a conscience and having the nerve to raise an objection when something doesn't seem fair. These texts also present a model of leadership that teaches that even the most venerated person in a religious tradition—in this case, Moses—doesn't know the right answer to every question and can't simply rely on whatever message he or she has delivered on behalf of God in the past. Moses here shows us that a good leader isn't a tyrant and isn't dogmatic. A good leader isn't threatened by a fair challenge either, and is willing to take the time to seek help and be open to new ideas that might even change the rules.

From Moses, God, Mahlah, Noah, Hoglah, Milcah, and Tirtzah, as well as from the men who brought the second appeal to the inheritance laws, we learn not only that good law is responsive to reasonable challenges, but also that it is responsive to *stories*. Law is an important part of the Torah, and of Moses' work. But *story* is equally important, and it is the specifics of a story that sometimes lead to the questioning of a law. This is what happened with Tzelophehad's daughters. Their specific story pointed out gaps in the existing law, and the justice of their claim caused even God to reconsider the law. What we learn here is that story and law are meant to have a reciprocal and mutually responsive relationship, and the same is true for questions and law. Even divine law exists within a framework of an ongoing relationship with humanity.

So if the law can change, can it change in *any* which way? I don't think that's what these passages from the Torah are trying to teach. The law changes in response to appeals for change *based on claims of justice*. The five daughters come to Moses and say, "Why should our father's name disappear from his clan because he had no son?"[8] In so many words, they're saying, "Hey, this law isn't fair! Why should it be that way?" Similarly the tribal heads who brought the second appeal framed it in the form of a complaint that some of the consequences of the new law would be unfair. The changes in the law that are made seek to expand justice, and to remedy injustice where it has previously existed in the law. *The truth* is

7. Klitsner, *Subversive Sequels in the Bible*, xxiii–xxv.

8. Num 27:4, *NIV.*

admissible as evidence when one is appealing the rightness of a particular law. If the truth is that there's something unfair going on because of the law, that claim deserves serious consideration. And we—mere mortals that we are, flaws and all—are the ones whom God relies upon to bring these questions and appeals based on truth and the demands of justice.

This kind of reciprocal relationship between God and the people goes all the way back to the modeling presented to us in Genesis 18, when God tells Abraham of God's plans to destroy the wicked cities of Sodom and Gomorrah. Abraham begins challenging God's plan on the basis of whether or not it is just, and starts asking God whether God will destroy the cities entirely if there are even fifty righteous people living there amongst the tens of thousands of evildoers. Famously, God grants that the cities will be spared if there should happen to be fifty such people living there, and then Abraham bargains that number down to ten. The crucial line of dialogue in the entire back-and-forth is when Abraham asks God point-blank the essential question on his mind: "Will the Judge of all the earth not do what is just?"[9] It's this sort of question, and the chutzpah it takes to ask it even of the Almighty One, that pierces to the heart of God, causing God to reconsider divine plans and laws.

What we can learn from Tzelophehad's daughters and Moses is that laws will be challenged from time to time on the basis of their failure to create justice, and that it's our obligation to take these challenges seriously. When these challenges come, it is our duty, like Moses, to consult with a Higher Power in asking whether the law needs to change to expand the circle of justice wider. For Moses and the Hebrew prophets, consulting with a Higher Power sometimes involved a private conversation with the Deity. In our era, and especially outside the world of traditional religion, we can still consult with a Higher Power, whether it be conscience, our own conception of God, or some other Source of Ultimate Truth. This is true in the arena of civil law as well as religious law.

If we consider for a moment the many times that the American founding legal documents have been challenged and then changed on the basis of complaints of injustice, either via written amendments or court interpretation, we see a living example of the Tzelophehad's Daughters Principle at work. The Declaration of Independence states that "all men are created equal," though the Constitution expressed this legal principle

---

9. Gen 18:25. Translation mine.

quite narrowly by giving the vote only to certain white males, enshrining slavery of African-Americans into law as well. As we all know, the idea of who should be considered included in the word "men" as it appears in the Declaration has undergone several expansions.

Equal rights, particularly voting rights, were first expanded to include the white males who were initially excluded—those who didn't happen to own property. Then came the vote for African-Americans following the Civil War, and then women's suffrage in the 1920s. In the mid-twentieth century, failure to implement the Declaration's expanded definition of the word "men," especially in the Southern states, led to the civil rights movement. One of the most effective signs that black men carried in protest marches simply said, in large letters, "I am a man." That sign was a succinct appeal to change the status quo, confronting the existing Jim Crow laws and abusive practices in the South with a complaint of injustice.

From a feminist perspective, the very fact that the Declaration used the word "men" and not "people" continues to rankle. Perhaps the limited male language throughout our founding US documents will one day be changed on the basis of a challenge yet to come. Nevertheless, since 1776 the definition of who is included among the class of humans who are deemed "created equal" has expanded dramatically, so much so that a person who might have been a slave 150 years ago has now become president, and in order to become president he had to compete fiercely to defeat a political challenge from someone who, because of her gender, wouldn't have been allowed to vote less than one hundred years ago. And this has become part of the mythic narrative that we tell ourselves about America: that this is the country of ever-expanding inclusion, equality, and freedom. This story helps us put America's early and unjust treatment of people of color and women into a hopeful framework, one that trusts that where injustices remain on the basis of status or identity, our society will eventually continue to expand its definitions of equality.

The episodes involving Tzelophehad's daughters present us with the same opportunity to apply this dynamic and reciprocal approach to religious law. I only feel qualified to speak on Jewish religious law, but I believe that the general ideas I have to share could be applied to other traditions too. Let me share my thoughts by way of a story. A couple of years ago I was invited to be part of an interfaith panel of clergy at the local community college. The college had just gone through a very painful incident involving graffiti vandalism attacking the gay/lesbian/transgender community. The walls of several buildings had been spray-painted with biblical verse citations that specifically condemn certain homosexual acts. The purpose of the panel was to invite gay-friendly clergy to speak about how they understand their own religious traditions to support and affirm the equality of gay and lesbian relationships.

During my presentation, I chose to talk about Tzelophehad's daughters. I explained that it was this model of Jewish law that I have come to embrace—a model that is open to challenges based on complaints of injustice. I explained that I had listened to dozens of personal stories about how the few passages in the Hebrew Bible condemning certain forms of male homosexual activity had led to countless acts of exclusion and condemnation resulting not only in tremendous suffering, but also at times in violence against innocent people. I also explained how there were other Jewish legal, ethical, and spiritual concepts that were at stake in religious questions about homosexuality, and that one of those concepts was the importance of nurturing and supporting sacredness (*kedushah* in Hebrew) in the various forms that it takes in our world. I could plainly see *kedushah* in the loving, committed relationships of two men or two women, and it felt wrong for me to participate in a pattern of religious expression that would suppress or refuse to respect that *kedushah*.

Recognizing, as discussed in chapter 6, that the truth and insight of the Torah represents only a *partial* truth, in my approach to Judaism I invite a dialogue between the truth I have witnessed and the words of the Torah, especially when there is conflict between the two. *The truth I have witnessed is that there is the same potential for love, commitment, mutual sharing, healthy family building, and spiritual growth in gay relationships as in straight.* Another truth I have witnessed is the cruelty inflicted by people brandishing Bibles and other holy books while they condemn homosexuality, which they don't really comprehend. Following the practice of my own denomination's approach to Judaism (i.e., Reconstructionism), I've studied Judaism's legal and interpretive traditions on the subject of homosexuality and I've had a constructive internal dialogue between Jewish texts and the truth that I've witnessed. The founder of the Reconstructionist movement, Rabbi Mordecai Kaplan, wrote:

> The modern Jew cannot . . . look to the Torah as a source of authority, in the sense that whatever it permits is right and what-

ever it forbids is wrong. He [or she] reverses the process and says: *Whatever is right should be incorporated in our Torah, and whatever is wrong should be eliminated from our Torah.* Inasmuch as no [one] can know, merely on the basis of personal experience, what is right and wrong in every situation, the traditional standards of right and wrong cherished by our people, and the institutions sanctioned by the Torah as aids to spiritual discipline, can and should be regarded with reverence, and should be observed, wherever experience has not challenged their validity. But we must not cling to the standards of the past, if they work mischief in the present.[10]

The appeal to truth that emanates from the gay community to be treated equally, to be affirmed and included fully, and to have gay marriages sanctified and recognized by religious and civic institutions is so clearly just that it *commands* me to do right action. I cannot let an inflexible passage or two of a text, even one sacred to me, become the reason why I commit harmful and damaging action and deny the sacredness that is present in same-sex as well as opposite-sex committed relationships. Like Tzelophehad's daughters' words, the words of God's gay sons and daughters are just, and I follow a new legal judgment on this matter.

***

At this point, I feel compelled to say a few words about a challenge I can imagine some of my friends in the Jewish community posing to me. I've written that the Torah's passages about Moses and Tzelophehad's daughters present us with a model of Divine law being open to revision and change in the context of a human-Divine dialogue, and I've asserted that that way of looking at the Torah's laws isn't generally taught from the pulpit. Some of my rabbinic colleagues might argue, however, that the traditional system of Jewish law that was developed by the ancient rabbis represents precisely the kind of living legal relationship between God and the Jewish people that the Tzelophehad's daughters texts present. They could rightly point out that this system of Jewish law, known as *halakhah*, has changed and reshaped Jewish law countless times in response to the shifting social, political, and economic circumstances of different historical moments.

---

10. Kaplan, *The Future of the American Jew*, 382. Italics are the author's.

In response, I would say that I think something different is going on in the Torah's texts about Tzelophehad's daughters. Their story models a kind of legal covenant between people and God that includes the right of *anyone* to directly seek a change in Torah law itself, based on a sincere appeal to fairness and an observation that there is a flaw in the existing law. The *halakhic* system, on the other hand, empowers only rabbis to consider making changes in Jewish law, and only under specifically defined extraordinary circumstances could these rabbis directly overturn, or uproot, a Torah commandment. Today in the Orthodox world, the *halakhic* system doesn't permit a wide range of legal change. Much of the innovation going on in Orthodox *halakhah* today deals with questions concerning new technologies that pose legal dilemmas that have never existed before. The rabbis of the Conservative movement have shown significantly greater flexibility in their *halakhic* rulings and interpretations, though they also have shown a preference for *halakhic* changes that avoid directly overturning a Torah law.

In contrast to the *halakhic* model's strong preference for reinterpreting, but not overturning and overtly changing, the Torah's laws, the Tzelophehad's daughters story suggests an approach to religious law that assumes that from time to time there will be *change in the actual foundational laws of the tradition—in this case, the Laws of Torah, of Moses—in response to a direct appeal from average people.* The five sisters and Moses teach us that God listens to appeals based on claims of justice, and that even the Torah's laws are not meant to be a closed and settled matter. This implies a more grassroots and inclusive process of discussion and decision-making regarding the evolution of Jewish law than a traditional *halakhic* model offers, as well as the availability to the community of a kind of "amendment process" to the Jewish legal "Constitution"—the Torah—in which the laws of the Torah itself can be revised and changed without the exercise of creative (and sometimes exhausting) legal reinterpretation by rabbis.

I'm not suggesting that the Torah as a whole supports my interpretation of the implications of the Tzelophehad's daughters episodes. On the contrary, the great majority of passages in the Torah present the standard, traditional theological position that the Torah's laws are immutable. But, as we've discussed in previous chapters, the Torah is a multivocal text with different layers and intentional, paradoxical contradictions. The voices of

Tzelophehad's daughters and Moses in these passages deserve to be heard, and the model of religious law they suggest deserves to be given due consideration.

***

A final word on divine law and its capacity for revision or even its over-turning. Looking to the book of Ruth, we find a situation that gives much food for thought. The book of Ruth is set during the period of the first couple of centuries after the death of Moses, when the Israelites were living as a loose confederation of tribes in the Promised Land. This is often referred to as the period of the Judges—"Judges" being the name given to a series of heroic and wise chiefs and leaders who helped the Israelites during periodic crises, often leading them in battle against the other peoples that populated the Promised Land at that time. The time of the Judges was a time of instability for the Israelites. They had no unified leader and their political and military control of the Promised Land was partial. The Philistines proved to be a frequent adversary, and sometimes fighting erupted with neighboring small kingdoms as well. From time to time, war would break out between Israelite tribes too. This was the period before the twelve tribes were finally united, first under the temporary rule of King Saul, and then under the legendary rule of King David.

The book of Ruth is named for a Moabite woman, and the story begins in the land of Moab, which was just beyond the eastern border of the Promised Land, in territory found today in Jordan. A famine in the Land of Israel had spurred a migration of Israelites into Moab, where there was food, and Ruth had intermarried with an Israelite immigrant, the son of a woman called Naomi. Tragically, both Naomi's and Ruth's husbands die early deaths, and the two women find themselves at a crossroads. Naomi tells Ruth that she is going to return to the Land of Israel to her people, and she advises Ruth to return to her family clan in Moab. Ruth adamantly refuses to leave Naomi and tells her famously, "Don't urge me to leave you or to turn back from you. Where you go I will go, and where you stay I will stay. Your people will be my people and your God my God. Where you die I will die, and there I will be buried. May the Eternal deal with me, be it ever so severely, if anything but death separates you and me."[11]

11. Ruth 1:16–17, *NIV* (adapted).

Naomi allows Ruth to come to the Land of Israel with her, and thanks to Ruth the fortunes of both women quickly improve. Ruth goes gleaning in a wealthy Israelite's field and he takes notice of her beauty. By the story's end, Ruth and Boaz, the owner of the field, get married. Naomi and Ruth are no longer vulnerable to starvation and are reestablished in a stable family system. Ruth and Boaz have a son, Oved, who later becomes the father of Jesse, who in turn becomes the father of King David.

The story of Ruth has served as the biblical model for conversion to Judaism, and many people who have gone through the long process of study and participation in Jewish life that culminates in becoming a "Jew-by-choice" have held dear the words quoted above that Ruth spoke to Naomi. Ruth is also an extremely important figure in Judaism because she is a direct ancestor of King David. Judaism, especially once it became a rabbinic tradition, developed a powerful belief and hope that one day God would send a redeemer—the Messiah—who would end Jewish suffering and exile and bring an era of peace and justice to the whole world. The Messiah, the tradition teaches, will be a descendant of King David. So in Jewish tradition, Ruth, the Moabite who adopted the religion of Israel, is the mother of Judaism's greatest King and the direct ancestor of its long-awaited Messiah.

There's only one problem with all this. The Torah mandates that no Moabite can join the people of Israel, at least not at the time that Ruth did. Deut 23:4 states, "a Moabite shall not enter the community of the Eternal, even until the tenth generation none of them shall enter into the community of the Eternal forever."[12] The story of Ruth takes place well within the time frame of ten generations. Moshe Weinfeld and S. David Sperling write in their *Encyclopaedia Judaica* article on the book of Ruth: "Ruth's author effectively repeals the exclusion of Moabites (Deut 23:4) . . . Instead, the book of Ruth points to the precedent of the ancient worthies who built up the house of Israel by ignoring the letter of the law when the growth of the house of Israel was at stake."[13]

So striking is the violation of Deuteronomy's commandment excluding Moabites from the possibility of conversion that the rabbis of Talmud felt it necessary to offer an explanation to remove the apparent contradic-

12. Translation mine.
13. Weinfeld and Sperling, from their *Encyclopaedia Judaica* article, "Ruth, Book of."

tion. They argue that the exclusion only applied to Moabite *males* because the word the Torah used for "Moabites" in Hebrew is the male plural form.

I have two difficulties with this midrashic resolving of the contradiction between Deuteronomy and Ruth. The first is that the Torah generally uses the male plural form to include everyone, like so many other languages do. The Talmudic sages seem to me like they're resisting the radical message in the book of Ruth. The second, and bigger, problem I have is that the Hebrew Bible is richer and more compelling as a moral guide, in my opinion, with the contradiction between the book of Ruth and Deuteronomy left in place. In chapter 6 we examined Robert Alter's discussion of the "composite artistry" of Torah, as well as Judy Klitsner's concept of the Hebrew Bible's "subversive sequels," and these ideas are wonderfully showcased in the case of Deuteronomy and Ruth. The Hebrew Bible *intentionally* includes these different, and at times contradictory, stories, and in doing so it presents us with paradox and alternative ways of looking at a larger truth that is beyond simple description.

If we let the contradiction between Deuteronomy and Ruth just be, then we're left with a Hebrew Bible that gives us a wonderful gift. With the Deuteronomy text, it gives us law. "No Moabites allowed." (It's not the exclusion of Moabites that I'm saying is wonderful, but rather the *idea* of law and its importance for human society to function in a way that creates higher meaning.) Then, in Ruth, paradoxically the Hebrew Bible gives us a story that includes the disregarding of a law. The lesson we can draw by holding both texts in view is that, in the case of this story, there was another understanding of truth operating—one that even contradicted accepted law—that we are meant to pay attention to. Maybe that truth is the transcendent power of love; maybe it's the truth of Ruth's inner experience—I'm not sure—but she and Naomi and Boaz and the entire Israelite community who accept Ruth break a law, and thanks to their actions King David is born, and one day the redeeming Messiah will be born as well! The Hebrew Bible as it is, without any rabbinic interpretive maneuvers tidying up this particular contradiction, gives us such a powerful lesson. It asks us to take seriously both the claims of a legal tradition and the truth of the heart, the truth we find through human experience.

8

The Voice of Pain and Cruelty in Moses[1]

IN JEWISH PRACTICE, WE divide the Torah into fifty-four portions, called *parashiyot* in Hebrew (*parashah* is the singular). Every Shabbat (Sabbath) morning, we read one parashah. This has its parallel in Christian lectionaries, though something distinctive about Jewish worship is that we not only study and discuss the weekly parashah, but we chant it aloud during Shabbat services in its original Hebrew, according to a specific system of cantillation called "trope." Each autumn, we complete our journey through the Torah for the year, and then we start from the beginning once again. Sometime every summer we arrive at the parashah that I find the most painful in all of Torah—the one called *Matot* (Num 30:2—32:42).

The setting is as follows: the Israelites are in their fortieth and final year of wandering in the wilderness. They are getting close to the border of the Promised Land. Moses is drawing near to the end of his life. Just recently, the Israelites went through one of their many spiritual and moral failings during their wandering years. During an episode in which they came into contact with the Midianites and the Moabites, many of the Israelites joined up with these peoples and offered sacrifices to their gods, including the deity known as Ba'al-Pe'or. Male Israelites especially were tempted into this idolatry by Midianite and Moabite women who in-

---

1. The title of this chapter is inspired by Rabbi Michael Lerner's description of a voice of pain and cruelty in Torah that is present alongside the voice of God, in his book, *Jewish Renewal: A Path to Healing and Transformation.*

cluded cultic sex as part of their polytheistic worship. God became furious over their idolatry and caused a plague to break out among the Israelites, which killed twenty-four thousand people before it subsided.[2]

Chapter 31 of Numbers begins with God commanding Moses to "[t]ake vengeance on the Midianites for the Israelites."[3] God tells Moses that once he has completed this final assignment, it will be time for his life to come to an end. The parashah then reports the outcome of the Israelite attack on the Midianites:

> They fought against Midian, as the Eternal commanded Moses, and killed every man . . . The Israelites captured the Midianite women and children and took all the Midianite herds, flocks and goods as plunder. They burned all the towns where the Midianites had settled, as well as all their camps. They took all the plunder and spoils, including the people and animals, and brought the captives, spoils and plunder to Moses and Elazar the priest and the Israelite assembly at their camp on the plains of Moab, by the Jordan across from Jericho.
>
> Moses, Elazar the priest, and all the leaders of the community went to meet them outside the camp. Moses was angry with the officers of the army—the commanders of thousands and commanders of hundreds—who returned from the battle.
>
> "Have you allowed all the women to live?" he asked them. "They were the ones who followed Balaam's advice and enticed the Israelites to be unfaithful to the Eternal in the Peor incident, so that a plague struck the Eternal's people. Now kill all the boys. And kill every woman who has slept with a man, but save for yourselves every girl who has never slept with a man."[4]

Verses 17–18 are the ones I find the most troubling, in which Moses gives the order to kill all the males among the children as well as the females who are not virgins, regardless of their age.

God's intent, and Moses', appears to be utter genocide, including the mass murder of children. The only people who are to be spared are virginal girls. (In the Torah's era these girls were people who, as part of the aftermath of war, could be subsumed into the patriarchal clans of the conquering nation.) The idea here is that by means of mass slaughter the people of Midian should not exist anymore.

2. Num 25:1–9.

3. Num 31:1, *NIV.*

4. Num 31:7–18, *NIV* (adapted).

This Torah portion contrasts sharply with many other parts of the Hebrew Bible, in which God or God's prophet demands some measure of compassion and humane treatment for the Israelites' enemies, or for nations that have slid collectively into terrible evil. Remember back in Genesis, Abraham bargained with God in a bid to spare the people of the wicked cities Sodom and Gomorrah.[5] And in the book of Jonah, God scolds Jonah, the reluctant prophet to the city of Nineveh, for his lack of compassion and concern for the people living there. Bear in mind that Nineveh was part of the Assyrian Empire—the same brutal regime that at one point conquered and exiled ten of the twelve tribes of Israel. Even so, the canonizers of the Hebrew Bible preserved this story of God requiring a Hebrew prophet, Jonah, to try to help them.

The Torah also presents us with these words: "Do not despise an Egyptian, because you resided as foreigners in their country.[6]" This despite Egypt's outrageous cruelty and enslavement of the Israelites. Much later in the Hebrew Bible, the prophet Isaiah envisions two of the great empires that brutalized the Israelites one day joining Israel in worship of God, and God lovingly embracing them, saying, "In that day Israel will be the third, along with Egypt and Assyria, a blessing on the earth. The Eternal Almighty will bless them, saying, 'Blessed be Egypt my people, Assyria my handiwork, and Israel my inheritance.'"[7] These passages point to a morality and a spirituality of transcending vengeful retribution towards even one's worst enemies, in contrast to the God who commands vengeance and genocide, or the Moses who gets angry when his army has failed to carry out the genocide sufficiently—the Moses who would cry out to his soldiers, "What, you left the women and the kids alive?!"

Numbers 31 parallels the famous later biblical account of King Saul's failure to completely carry out another divine order to commit genocide, this time against the nation of Amalek. For his failure to "finish the job," God condemns Saul to lose his kingship and any future royal line.[8] There, the genocidal orders are even more explicit:

> [The Prophet] Samuel said to Saul, "I am the one the Eternal sent to anoint you king over his people Israel; so listen now to the mes-

5. See Gen 18:16–33.

6. Deut 23:8 in Jewish versions of the Bible; 23:7 in Christian versions. *NIV.*

7. Isa 19:24–25, *NIV* (adapted).

8. 1 Sam 15.

sage from the Eternal. This is what the Eternal Almighty says: 'I will punish the Amalekites for what they did to Israel when they waylaid them as they came up from Egypt. Now go, attack the Amalekites and totally destroy all that belongs to them. Do not spare them; put to death men and women, children and infants, cattle and sheep, camels and donkeys.'"[9]

Saul sent his army in with these orders and at the end of the slaughter the Israelite troops thought they had killed every single Amalekite, except one, their king, Agag. But the text says that Saul had pity on Agag and spared his life. The Israelite army also kept some of the choicest sheep and oxen as spoils, contradicting God's command. As a result of these violations, God informs the prophet Samuel that God has rejected Saul as king. Saul begs for a second chance, but it's too late. Samuel then has Agag brought before him, takes his sword and cuts Agag into pieces, thus completing the genocide of Amalek.[10]

But it turns out that the Amalekites were not wiped out with the execution of King Agag. They appear again as military adversaries in the Hebrew Bible during the reign of King David, and again in the book of Esther, in the form of the wicked Haman himself, said to be a descendant of Agag. How some Amalekites managed to survive Saul's annihilation is not explained, but many rabbis to this day claim that the lesson to be learned from this part of the Bible is that Saul's compassion was misplaced, and that we too should be wary of our impulse towards mercy in dealing with our bitterest enemies. Amalek's persistent presence as an avowed enemy led to a strand of rabbinic tradition that claims that Amalek continues to exist in every era, plotting to destroy the Jews, and that it is incumbent upon Jews not to repeat the mistake of allowing misplaced compassion to prevent us from annihilating the present-day "Amalekites" vigorously and without mercy whenever the opportunity arises.

Well over 2,500 years since the completion of the Torah, some notable Israeli rabbis with right-wing ideologies have advocated the idea that the Arabs or the Palestinians constitute the current incarnation of

9. 1 Sam 15:1–3, *NIV.*

10. Or so it seems. Rabbinic tradition developed the belief that Saul's failure to kill every last Amalakite resulted in the Amalekites continuing to live on throughout the ages. This has led to a traditional Jewish teaching that the arch enemies of the Jews throughout the ages have all been descendants of Amalek. More on the implications of this belief further along in this chapter.

Amalek, and that we as Jews are, or soon will be, morally required to ex-
terminate them.[11] On the Internet today, it is easy to find Jewish websites
that continue to identify Amalek with contemporary adversaries that the
modern State of Israel faces. If it's not the Palestinians who are the new incarnation of Amalek, then it's the Iranians, or Mahmoud Ahmadinajad in
particular, or the Arabs as a whole. (These writers often add hateful rhetoric towards their fellow Jews who have left-leaning views on the Israeli-
Palestinian conflict.) One kabbalistic website based in the northern Israeli
city of Tzfat (Safed), in response to the 2006 Israel-Hezbollah war, states:
"The Torah speaks of the tribe of *Amalek*. Historically, the tribe of Amalek
pathologically hated and wanted to destroy Israel. Today, although the
lines defining the cultural identities of the nations have been blurred, we
still suffer from the scourge of Amalek. Amalek is now a minority whose
death-obsessed ideology is polluting larger and larger segments of the
world's population. In the past, it has seeped through and manifested itself
as Haman, Hitler, Saddam Hussein, Hamas. Now it is Hizbullah."[12]

Expressing concern over this phenomenon, a rabbinical student at
the New York-based Orthodox seminary *Chovevei Torah* wrote the following about contemporary right-wing leaders in the Jewish or Israeli
community invoking Amalek in reference to their enemies:

> Even if most people would not invoke the commandment to de-
> stroy Amalek today, there are certainly those . . . who have ven-
> tured to do so. And there has been no dearth of similar, violent
> invocations in reference to the Palestinians, as well . . . The general
> consensus among today's Jewish community seems to be that our
> energies can and must be used to stop the perpetuation of geno-
> cidal activity occurring throughout the world, to become agents
> for peace, and to dismiss any contemporary comparisons to the
> biblical paradigm. But clearly there are difficult texts and teach-

11. Perhaps the best known of these public statements came from Rabbi Israel Hess
in the February 26, 1980, issue of Bar Ilan University's publication *Bat Kol*. Rabbi Hess
was subsequently dismissed from his position at the university. More recently, certain
leading Israeli rabbis have made statements supporting the killing of Arab civilians so
long as a state of war continues to exist, or calling for the extermination of Arabs. These
extremist statements have been met with condemnation by other Israeli rabbis, such as
David Hartman in Jerusalem, by various Orthodox leaders, and by Israeli politicians, to
be sure. Nevertheless, many Israelis worry that this kind of genocide-approving interpretation of these biblical texts is growing in popularity among the religious right in Israel.

12. Nadborny-Burgeman, "Ascent and the Terrorist War from Lebanon."

ings that remain in our tradition that must be remembered and reckoned with.[13]

As these examples make clear, texts in the Torah and the other books of the Hebrew Bible that depict God, Moses, or other leaders (Joshua comes to mind) carrying out the Divine will through acts of mass slaughter, including civilians and children, are being used in the here and now to justify religious acts of violence. These texts form the backbone of a dangerous theological movement among some on the Jewish religious right, including certain extremist groups among the settlements on the West Bank. This is a movement that dehumanizes its enemies and legitimizes violence against those who would seek to recognize the legitimacy of Palestinian statehood alongside Israel—a core element of the "two-state solution" that so many global political leaders have worked for in recent decades.

To be fair, this ideology is not embraced by many Israelis living in the West Bank, and the vast majority of settlers do not commit acts of violence against their Palestinian neighbors. But for a zealous minority on the Israeli far right, passion to fight "Amalek in our times" leads some devout and observant Jews to do things like carry out so-called price tag operations, which are acts of deliberate violence committed against Palestinians, carried out in response to Israeli government enforcement of laws designed to prevent the spontaneous erecting of illegal settlement outposts. When the Israeli army dismantles a group of shacks set up by Jewish extremists seeking to lay claim to a new West Bank hilltop, for example, these individuals make sure there's a "price tag" for the Palestinians to pay. Some adherents to this ideology have also threatened to use violence against Israeli military personnel or government officials who might one day be ordered to evacuate a settlement as part of a peace agreement with the Palestinians.[14] Yigal Amir justified his 1995 assassination of Israeli Prime Minister Yitzhak Rabin on the basis of Jewish sacred texts as understood through this kind of thinking. This movement continues

13. Yanklowitz, "Genocide in the Torah."

14. As just one example, the Israeli daily *Ha'aretz* reported on January 6, 2010, that Israel's Defense Minister, Ehud Barak, received a death threat from a far rightist Israeli Jewish group. The written death threat included the following messages: "If you think of destroying the settlements, you are mistaken, and I will kill you," and "I will harm you or your children, be careful. If not now, then when you are no longer a minister and have no security around you."

to manifest in religious proclamations such as this one in November 2009 reported in the Israeli newspaper *Ha'aretz*:

> a West Bank rabbi on Monday released a book giving Jews permission to kill Gentiles who threaten Israel. Rabbi Yitzhak Shapiro, who heads the Od Yosef Chai Yeshiva in the Yitzhar settlement, wrote in his book *The King's Torah* that even babies and children can be killed if they pose a threat to the nation. Shapiro based the majority of his teachings on passages quoted from the Bible, to which he adds his opinions and beliefs. "It is permissible to kill the Righteous among Nations even if they are not responsible for the threatening situation," he wrote . . . Several prominent rabbis, including Rabbi Yitzhak Ginzburg and Rabbi Yaakov Yosef, have recommended the book to their students and followers.[15]

In case it's not obvious, I have a huge problem with sacred texts (of any faith) that depict God or one of God's prophets ordering, approving, and rewarding acts of brutality, including mass conquest, genocide, violence against women, children, and civilians, or violence based on claims that some nation or people has become irreversibly "polluted" or evil and therefore must be completely exterminated. The Episcopal priest and noted writer Bishop John Shelby Spong recently published an entire book on these kinds of sacred texts within his religion, titled *The Sins of Scripture: Exposing the Bible's Texts of Hate to Reveal the God of Love*. He writes:

> Text by text I will seek to disarm those parts of the biblical story that have been used throughout history to hurt, denigrate, oppress, and even kill. I will set about to deconstruct the Bible's horror stories. But destruction is neither my aim nor my goal. I want above all else to offer believers a new doorway into the biblical story, a new way to read and to listen to this ancient narrative. I want to lead people beyond the sins of Scripture embedded in its "terrible texts" in order to make a case for the Bible as that ultimate shaper of the essence of our humanity and as a book that calls us to be something we have not yet become.[16]

I write this chapter with similar intentions. Borrowing language developed by Rabbi Michael Lerner, who has also addressed the potential

---

15. Excerpted from "*West Bank rabbi: Jews can kill gentiles who threaten Israel*," *Haaretz*, November 9, 2009.

16. Spong, *The Sins of Scripture*, 24–25.

for violence inherent in these kinds of sacred texts, henceforth I will refer to Bishop Spong's "terrible texts" as "texts of cruelty."

The text this chapter began with, Numbers 31, is one of the main Jewish sacred texts that promotes the idea of divinely commanded genocide, a concept that I find spiritually abhorrent and completely incompatible with the truth about what God is. Of course, Judaism has no monopoly on sacred texts that depict God endorsing brutality and cruelty towards the Other. Islam and Christianity both have the same thing going on with horrible real-world results.

At this time I'd like to present a few examples of texts of cruelty found in Christianity and Islam, in the hope of showing that all religions have a dark side, and in the hope that by examining the common features of religious texts of cruelty we stand a chance to learn something about how practitioners of all religions can find a way to stop using religion to hurt rather than to heal. I'll start by turning to examples of texts of cruelty within Islam, though before I do so I feel the need to offer a disclaimer. Because I'm all too aware of the fearmongering and misrepresentations of Islam that have permeated mass media in the United States ever since 9/11, I feel a responsibility to state unequivocally that Islam-bashing is not my intent, nor is Islamophobia an ideology I support. As a congregational rabbi I have stood up with other local clergy more than once to lend support to members of the local Muslim community in the face of this anti-Muslim hateful rhetoric. My agenda here is well expressed by the words of the Islamic studies professor Omid Safi, who writes: "There are passages in both the Qur'an and the Bible that preach mutual respect and coexistence, and in both Scriptures there are also passages that justify chauvinism and even violence. The question for us is how to approach any Scripture in a way that is both historically informed and intellectually honest. This challenge is harder than most of the faithful are willing to admit—at least publicly."[17]

So I'll begin with a text that is, unfortunately, oft-quoted by Islam-bashers. Without sharing their bigoted agenda, I hope to show how this text, from the sacred literature known as Hadith, is being put in service of an ideology that demonizes Jews and justifies the targeting of Israeli civilians for violence. Alan Johnson writes, "The Hamas charter extols the wisdom of al-Bukhari's canonical Hadith: 'The hour of judgment shall

17. Safi, *Memories of Muhammad*, 214.

not come until the Muslims fight the Jews and kill them, so that the Jews hide behind trees and stones, and each tree and stone will say: O Muslim, O servant of Allah, there is a Jew behind me, come and kill him.'"[18] Regardless of whatever context this Hadith comes from, it presents an image of the universal Jew as demonic and in some sense unnatural. When even the trees and rocks have become allied in the fight against "the Jew," you know you're looking at a text that not only dehumanizes its target group, but that fantasizes about a world in which the Jews have no place to hide. Israelis and Jews worldwide are easily re-traumatized by this kind of rhetoric given the memory of the Nazi Holocaust. Even if an Islamic studies scholar were to argue that, in its original historical context, this passage isn't as cruel as it seems, we are left in the present day with the fact that a political movement like Hamas is putting this text in service of an ideology that does advocate a form of religious supremacy and that engages in violence against civilians on a routine basis.

There are many passages in the Qur'an and Hadith literature that express tolerance and respect for Judaism and Christianity, and intellectual honesty demands that we acknowledge that those passages sit alongside verses that denigrate other religions or depict God engaging in punishing violence against the Other. With regards to the more problematic sacred texts in Islam, I've attended presentations in which I've heard Muslim clerics or presenters present apologetics for these texts, and I have found these arguments as unconvincing and disappointing as similar arguments I've heard made by Christian and Jewish teachers. The Muslim reformer Irshad Manji writes in response to these apologetics, "I've read the scholarship that explains these verses 'in their context,' and I think there's a fancy dance of evasion going on."[19]

One of the things that worries me about this "dance of evasion" is that it makes it all but impossible for reformers from within Islam to try to speak candidly about this issue or advocate for change. Insisting that one's sacred texts are perfect and therefore incapable of promoting injustice or cruelty also provides cover for those within a religious tradition who want to use sacred texts of cruelty for the express purpose of demonizing the

18. Johnson, "Hamas and Antisemitism," *The Guardian*, May 15, 2008. Hadith is a category of Islamic teachings representing sayings attributed to or approved by the Prophet Muhammad.

19. Manji, *The Trouble with Islam Today*, 43.

Other. Some of the educational practices that go on routinely in many Muslim countries illustrate this problem. For instance, as recently as 2008, Saudi Arabian official school textbooks for 8th graders stated, "As cited in Ibn Abbas: The apes are Jews, the people of the Sabbath, while the swine are Christians, the infidels of the communion of Jesus."[20] This is only one of many examples of inflammatory passages in the official Saudi school books.

Sura 8 of the Qur'an presents an example of God describing warfare between people who are "on God's side" and people who are "opposing God"—the kind of black-and-white thinking that we also find among Jewish and Christian fundamentalists. This passage also condemns "unbelievers" to the fires of hell: "I will cast terror into the hearts of those who disbelieve. Therefore strike off their heads and strike off every fingertip of them. This is because they acted adversely to Allah and His Messenger; and whoever acts adversely to Allah and His Messenger—then surely Allah is severe in requiting (evil). This—taste it, and (know) that for the unbelievers is the chastisement of fire."[21] The passage continues as follows: "O you who believe! when you meet those who disbelieve marching for war, then turn not your backs to them. And whoever shall turn his back to them on that day—unless he turn aside for the sake of fighting or withdraws to a company—then he, indeed, becomes deserving of Allah's wrath, and his abode is hell; and an evil destination shall it be."[22]

Even taking into consideration that in a proper context these verses may be referring only to specific historical moments in the past, or even assuming that this text only advocates defensive warfare, these words still present us with a God who divides the world into "believers" and "unbelievers," and who slays and consigns to hell the unbelievers. My hope is that honest discussion about the problems of texts of cruelty will expand and become ever more acceptable in mainstream Islam. From my position as a Jewish-American whose understanding of Islam is thinner than my understanding of Judaism or Christianity, it seems to me that this kind of open discussion about texts of cruelty exists mainly on the margins of

20. "2008 Update: Saudi Arabia's Curriculum of Intolerance," from the Center for Religious Freedom of the Hudson Institute with the Institute for Gulf Affairs, 5. The quote was taken from the textbook *Monotheism, Eighth Grade,* Kingdom of Saudi Arabia, Ministry of Education, Education Development, 1428–29; 2007–8, 42.

21. Sura 8, vv. 12b–14, *Shakir.*

22. Sura 8, vv. 15–16 *Shakir.*

Islam, though I would welcome being shown evidence that it has become more mainstream than I realize.

***

Turning to Christianity, we also find texts of cruelty. Numerous New Testament passages denigrate the Other (in many cases, the Jews), and passages in the book of Revelation depict an apocalyptic final battle between the followers of Jesus and all non-believers. In a chapter in his book titled "The Bible and Anti-Semitism," Bishop Spong cites what he calls a "favorite text of anti-Semitism" deriving from the Gospel of Matthew.[23] He writes, "In this narrative the Jewish crowd, prior to the crucifixion, is portrayed as responding to Pilate's plea of [Jesus'] innocence by saying, 'His blood be on us and on our children.' (Matt 27:25)"[24] Spong also writes, "John's Gospel quotes Jesus as saying that the Jews are 'from your father the devil, and you choose to do your father's desires' (8:44). Whenever the phrase 'the Jews' is used in John's Gospel, there is a pejorative undertone."[25] Spong's intention is to urge Christians to take responsibility for these texts and to be honest about the damage they have done and continue to do to the Jewish community and to Jewish-Christian relations.

Turning to the book of Revelation, we find a bloodbath in which the Other—the "unbelievers"—are mass-murdered and thus the earth is finally cleansed. Here we find a God who not only engages in killing on a cataclysmic scale, but who tortures as well.[26] Jesus, who in the Gospels put up no violent resistance to the Romans' cruelty, here becomes a cosmic warrior, riding a white horse, a sword coming from his mouth and slaughtering the armies of unbelievers by the millions.[27]

This description of a great slaughter set to take place at the end of days is frightening enough as a piece of fantasy literature, but terrifying in a very real sense when used by certain Christian fundamentalist leaders to advocate for reckless and extremist political and military policies here and now. Christian apocalyptic texts of cruelty have come to form

23. Spong, *The Sins of Scripture*, 185.

24. Ibid.

25. Ibid.

26. Rev 9:1–6.

27. Rev 19:11–21.

a pillar of right-wing conservative politics in the United States, and they are frequently put in service by religious leaders who, in many books, sermons, radio and TV programs, advocate for American military aggression against a number of different nations whom these religious leaders identify with various "baddies" in their biblically based end times script. Some Christian leaders who subscribe to this ideology also use these texts to advocate for the mass deportation of West Bank Palestinians—ethnic cleansing—in order to make space for the influx of Jews they believe will, in the near future, be moving to the biblical Land of Israel in fulfillment of scriptural prophecy.

Consider also the millions of Christian kids being brought up on the pop culture fantasy of the *Left Behind* series of books by Tim LaHaye and Jerry Jenkins, in which true believers are "raptured" and the unbelievers comprising the rest of humanity are left behind on earth and given the chance to embrace Christian belief or face eternal damnation. The drama takes place amidst global chaos, upheaval, and violence, in which other religions of the world and international organizations that promote religious coexistence, like the UN, are all tools of the anti-Christ. This work of fiction (and companion video games and other entertainment media) offers an interpretation of the biblical books of Revelation, Ezekiel, Isaiah, and Daniel that divides the world into "us and them," and portrays God as an author of cruelty on a mass scale. One of my friends who is a Methodist minister once described this strand of Christianity to me as the "Jesus comes back and kicks ass" version of his religion, which he finds so frightening that he makes a point of morally objecting to it in his ministry.

All of these are examples of monotheistic religions drawing on sacred texts that depict God and/or a central prophetic figure (Moses, Muhammad, Jesus) commanding or presiding over mass killing or torture on the basis of a Divine decision that has judged the victims of this violence to be enemies of God who are evil beyond redemption. All over the world today, certain ministers, imams, or rabbis use these kinds of texts to advocate for acts of violence in the name of God. This is the kind of religious use of texts of cruelty that brought us the Crusades and the Inquisition, and more recently: 9/11; Palestinian suicide bombings; the Taliban's treatment of women; the Israeli extremist Baruch Goldstein's massacre of Muslims at prayer; Serbian war crimes against Bosnian Muslims; and the murder of doctors in the United States who perform abortions—to name but a few examples of a much longer list. The theologian and writer Karen Armstrong calls this phenomenon "the fundamentalist tendency to use mythology as a blueprint for action," and she describes this kind of behavior as "terrifying."[28]

I see the great violence that is being done worldwide, cloaked in the garb of religious piety and fueled by certain unambiguously violent sacred texts, and I choose not to be a party to it—not even passively—by failing to condemn the explicit teachings of these passages in our various sacred texts. Someone who has written beautifully on the need to confront religious texts of cruelty with honesty and moral courage is Rabbi Michael Lerner, who addressed this topic in his 1994 book, *Jewish Renewal*. In a chapter called "The Struggle between Two Voices of God in Torah," Lerner put it this way: "In every generation those who have heard the voice of God have also heard the voice of cruelty, violence, and pain, and have often attributed that voice to God as well. The compilers of the Torah were no exception—they were human beings who struggled to hear the voice of God but who were simultaneously terrified to stay connected to the message of radical freedom that they heard. They retreated at times into hearing the more familiar messages, ones that seemed more congruent with their worlds of pain and oppression."[29]

The genuine voice of God is, for Lerner, always the voice of transformation and healing[30]—it is the voice that urges us towards the "defeat of cruelty."[31] God is "the Force in the world that makes possible the transformation of that which is to that which ought to be."[32] The truly Divine voice inspires awe for the natural world we are a part of and motivates us to work to bring down oppressive social and economic structures that demean human beings anywhere.[33] Lerner sees the authentic Divine voice in the Torah in the story of the liberation from slavery and in the commandments to treat the stranger, the vulnerable person, and the outsider with justice and kindness.[34] He writes, "Torah is filled with the voice of God...

28. Armstrong, *The Battle for God*, 348.

29. Lerner, *Jewish Renewal*, 31.

30. Ibid., xviii.

31. Ibid., 26.

32. Ibid., xviii.

33. Lerner, *Jewish Renewal*. See especially chapter 1, "Cruelty Is Not Destiny."

34. Ibid. See especially chapter 1, "Cruelty Is Not Destiny."

a voice of compassion and transcendence. But it is also filled with another voice, which mirrors human distortion and accumulated pain . . . Our job is to distinguish the one from the other."[35] And later, he adds: "I confront these [texts of cruelty] . . . not to judge those who adopted [them], but to say in the most unequivocal terms: *This is not the voice of God,* but the voice of pain and cruelty masquerading as the voice of God."[36]

I couldn't agree more or say it more powerfully. It *is* our job to distinguish between whether we are hearing the voice of God in the Torah (or the New Testament, the Qur'an, etc.), or whether we are encountering an instance of the voice of "pain and cruelty masquerading as the voice of God." We *must* use our consciences and our connection with the Divine within to do our best to discern. And when our heart of hearts tells us that a particular passage or text is teaching us to perpetuate a legacy of pain and cruelty in the pious packaging of religiosity, it is our moral duty to say so. It is also our ethical obligation to let our coreligionists know when we think they have grabbed hold of an expression of pain and cruelty in our sacred texts and are using it to behave unjustly in the name of God.

Some traditionalists attempt to delegitimize this stance towards the Bible (or any religion's sacred text) by dismissing it as "picking and choosing," which they say isn't the same thing as authentically following one's religion. To authentically follow one's religion means to obey the authoritative texts and accepted interpretations, they claim. To this argument I reply that religion is at its most dangerous when it is made up of *followers* rather than responsible and conscientious *participants.*

The new vision that I hope will emerge in all religious traditions is the vision of religious communities made up of *participants* who take moral responsibility for the actions done by their members and in their name. It's a vision of religious life that is guided by the same principle that doctors swear to with their Hippocratic Oath: in matters of religion, *first do no harm.* I'm talking about religious participants who come to their religion to seek out the voice of God wherever it appears in texts, rituals, ethics, and community, but who also come with an awareness that blind obedience to any received tradition is a moral choice that can cause tremendous destruction and harm.

35. Ibid., 87.
36. Ibid., 92. Italics are the author's.

Ultimately, it's part of the human condition that each of us *has to* "pick and choose," including who or what one gives authority to. To give unquestioning authority to a text or to a particular tradition of interpreting that text is a choice that carries moral consequences. Sometimes the consequence is millions of people agreeing that cruelty towards others can be justified if the sacred text, or the cleric one chooses to follow, insists that cruelty is what God demands of us.

Irshad Manji, addressing her fellow Muslims, writes, "if we don't open our eyes to patterns of prejudice [within our religion], then we can easily feed a system that treats millions of God's creatures as inferior, even occult, beings."[37] Her call for independent thinking and critical evaluation of sacred texts by Muslims applies equally to Judaism, Christianity, or any religion. Dr. Robert Eisen, an Orthodox Jew and the Director of Judaic Studies at George Washington University, once put it like this: "There is no 'I was just following orders' excuse for crimes committed in the name of one's religion."[38] God gave us consciences and the ability to think critically. To choose to set these gifts aside and simply follow a text or a sage who instructs us to commit acts of cruelty is a dangerous moral choice. To choose to defend or justify a sacred text's depiction of God as an author of genocide or brutality is also a moral and spiritual choice. It is our moral duty to say of these texts, along with Rabbi Lerner, *This is not the voice of God.*

Dr. Ron Kraybill is a Mennonite Christian who writes and teaches on conflict transformation with a particular focus on religion's role as a source of violence as well as a resource for peace. He writes that "most people of faith have little awareness of the dimensions of their own traditions that are most commonly used to justify destructive actions and attitudes towards others . . . People of faith have an obligation to become informed about the full extent of the damage done in their name. Survival of our world requires 'an end to assumed innocence'" on the part of religions.[39]

So Moses teaches us something I don't think he or the tradition intended to teach us in Numbers 31. He teaches us that we have a moral

37. Manji, *The Trouble with Islam Today*, 66.

38. I heard him teach these words during a course I took at the 2006 Summer Peacebuilding Institute of Eastern Mennonite University. The course was called, "Religion: Source of Conflict, Resource for Peace."

39. From my notes at the 2006 Summer Peacebuilding Institute of Eastern Mennonite University course, "Religion: Source of Conflict, Resource for Peace."

responsibility to question his instructions, whether the instructions are coming from him, or purportedly from God. We have a duty to ask, "Is this text giving voice to divine truth or human distortion?" This is a teaching that will no doubt offend some. So be it. I'd rather offend some than stand in affirmation of texts in my tradition that try to suggest a God who is something other than the Source of healing, goodness, and transformation in our lives. With all the brutality, violence, xenophobia, warmongering, and cruelty being carried out in the name of the monotheistic religions today, I think the moral onus is on those who would insist on a traditional belief in "perfect," "infallible," or 100 percent divinely revealed sacred texts to justify the human costs of their approach.

Moses teaches us, unintentionally, of the moral importance of being *responsible participants* of our religions—discerning partakers who don't follow a tradition as a whole blindly, but who take seriously the ethical duty to weigh whether the teaching that's coming from the tradition is one that affirms what our hearts and consciences confirm to be the truth. When tradition inevitably falls short, this doesn't mean our religion has become worthless. There's no need to throw out the baby with the bath water. It simply means, as Rabbi Lerner has so wisely articulated, that sometimes our sacred texts and traditions reflect our ancestors' legacy of pain and distortion rather than the sacred Truth. Irshad Manji draws similar conclusions and advocates that her fellow Muslims embrace a willingness to regard the Qur'an as imperfect, while reclaiming and utilizing in new ways the process of *ijtihad,* "the Islamic tradition of independent reasoning,"[40] to confront and counter those mullahs and imams who cite sacred texts to advocate for cruelty and violence.[41]

What is needed is an approach to religious life that affirms that God is present in all peoples, in each individual, and in all religious traditions. Distortion and spiritual error are *also* present in all religions and all sacred texts. In order to help use religion as a force for peace building and for the honoring and affirmation of life everywhere, we need to learn to be honest about our sacred texts and our traditions. As Dr. Robert Eisen taught me, "If you are not prepared to be honest with your own tradition, you are not prepared to be a peacemaker."[42]

40. Manji, *The Trouble with Islam Today,* 50.

41. Ibid., chapters 2 and 3.

42. From my notes at the 2006 Summer Peacebuilding Institute of Eastern Mennonite

I know that as soon as someone makes the case for treating one's religion and its sacred texts as valuable but flawed, some traditionalists quickly make the accusation that this stance is moral relativism. This isn't correct. Dissenting from sacred texts of cruelty is the act of someone who has the firm belief that part of ultimate Truth is that God doesn't teach or support cruelty. There *is* ultimate Truth, and the Torah (as well as other religions' sacred texts) have captured and profoundly expressed *parts* of that Truth imperfectly. The great danger with religion is that sacred texts include elements of ultimate Truth alongside falsehoods that are presented as Truth. Truth is real and it is the Truth for everyone. It's just not recorded in perfect and total form in anybody's sacred book.

***

If Moses unintentionally teaches us about the dangers of blind obedience to religious authority, what then do we do with our various religions' texts of cruelty? We can't in good conscience, I feel, carry on reading and studying our texts of cruelty without some comment or intervention. I agree with the contemporary Jewish philosopher Judith Plaskow, who in a 1994 essay about texts of cruelty in the Torah asked, "What do we do with hard texts? What do we do, when as individuals or communities, we find ourselves faced with texts that not only express values we no longer share, but that seem to support and encourage hatred, oppression, and violence in the world?"[43] Responding to her own question, she later writes, "[I don't] think we can interpret [hard texts] away. In reading the Torah aloud each week as sacred text, we receive it ever again in the present, hearing it directly and unadorned . . . There is no easy way to escape or ignore the hard places in Torah."[44] So what are our options for dealing with these texts?

In an essay titled, "Passages in Religious Texts Advocating Violence and Genocide," Vladmir Tomek makes the following observation and proposal: "Only religion can justify the destruction of human life sanctimoniously. It is a serious mistake to downplay the problem of religious violence in 'sacred' texts. The violence-of-God tradition in the Hebrew Scriptures, the Christian New Testament, and the Qur'an must be under-

University course, "Religion: Source of Conflict, Resource for Peace."

43. Plaskow, "Dealing with the Hard Stuff," 57.

44. Ibid.

stood and challenged if we are to have any realistic hope of building a peaceful and tolerant world. Change, of course, is profoundly difficult for those who believe in God's inspiration of the authors, and the inerrancy of the entire text."[45] Tomek adds, "In religions where images of violence, warfare, and martial exploits are prominent (such as in the Abrahamic religions), the elimination of all passages in the holy texts that incite to violence would certainly go some way towards rectifying the situation."[46]

Is this step—the elimination of texts of cruelty from all our sacred texts—a good idea? Is it realistically possible? I don't know. When I was a rabbinical student at the Reconstructonist Rabbinical College in Philadelphia, I took a required course on Christianity taught by a Methodist minister and scholar, Rev. Dr. Hal Taussig. He shared with our class a story about a series of discussions that the members of his church and the members of a local synagogue had had together. The synagogue rented the sanctuary on Fridays and Saturdays from Rev. Taussig's church, and the two congregations had a warm relationship. Both were liberal congregations with strong commitments to social justice.

One year, Rev. Taussig and one of the synagogue's rabbis led an interfaith course that ended up examining anti-Jewish polemics in the New Testament. The course attracted many people from both congregations, and the Christian participants found themselves stunned into a new level of awareness of just how negative many of the statements made about Jews in the New Testament are. They also learned about how, over the centuries, these negative characterizations of the Jews in the Christian Scriptures were used over and over again to justify brutality, violence, and murder against Jews. Jewish participants shared how uncomfortable and distrusting these particular Christian texts continued to make them feel even now.

By the time the course had ended, a group of Rev. Taussig's congregants began asking why their church continues to read the offending passages aloud in services, year after year, as well as in Bible study and other forums. "Shouldn't we strike these anti-Semitic texts out of our tradition?" they asked. Rev. Taussig took this question to the rabbi and the Jewish participants of the class, and this was their response: *No, you must leave these texts in your Scriptures. Leave them there and make a commitment*

45. Tomek, "Passages Advocating Violence and Genocide in Religious Texts."
46. Ibid.

to take responsibility for the violent and dangerous uses they have served and, in some parts of the Christian world, continue to serve. Discuss them, educate about them, find new approaches to responding to them. Read them aloud in church and openly disagree with them, refuse to accept their claims about the Jews, and model that behavior to other Christians. The Jewish group went on to say that they were quite aware that the Torah and other Jewish sacred writings had plenty of examples of texts of cruelty too, and that they felt it was their responsibility to treat those texts in the same way they were advising Rev. Taussig's congregation.

This is an approach I call *choosing to name our religious texts of cruelty and learn from them.* A text of cruelty becomes an opportunity to study an example of how one's religious ancestors made spiritual errors—and even to make a moral accounting of any harm that one's religion has inflicted over the years, or continues to inflict while using texts of cruelty as a justification. Texts of cruelty can unintentionally teach us to become better moral and spiritual people if we disarm them of their capacity to hurt or kill, to poison the mind, and then go on to use their existence as a call to repair the error in our tradition by embracing Truth instead. Often, we can turn to other sacred texts in our own tradition that "testify against" a particular text of cruelty, though we shouldn't require that contradictory texts be present within our religion in order to dissent from a text of cruelty. The Truth is the Truth is the Truth, whether one's religion managed to get it right or not.

By choosing to name our religious texts of cruelty and learn from them, we can stay in relationship with the Moses and the God of Numbers 31 without collaborating in the evil—and I mean *evil*—that this chapter attempts to teach. Moses still remains our teacher, only in Numbers 31 he unintentionally teaches us to be people who stand against any claim that God is genocidal or sanctions the murder of children and other innocents. And more importantly, the Moses of Numbers 31 can teach us to stand up against religious or national leaders who seek to hurt or kill others "in God's name" by citing this or other similar sacred texts.

***

Sometimes a religion "tames" some of its harshest texts by means of accepted interpretations that reshape texts of cruelty into something less disturbing. This is exactly what the ancient rabbis chose to do in certain cases with Torah passages that advocate cruelty. They used their Talmudic interpretive methods to eviscerate certain brutal passages of Torah of their ruthlessness, taming these texts by using their religious authority to assert that these verses actually meant something very different than what a plain reading would indicate.

A well-known example of this rabbinic upending of a disturbing Torah text is known in Hebrew as *ben sorer u-moreh,* "the case of the stubborn and rebellious son." An early rabbinic legal work, the Mishnah, includes an interpretation of the "true" meaning of the Torah's verses, Deut 21:18–21, which state: "If someone has a stubborn and rebellious son who does not obey his father and mother and will not listen to them when they discipline him, his father and mother shall take hold of him and bring him to the elders at the gate of his town. They shall say to the elders, 'This son of ours is stubborn and rebellious. He will not obey us. He is a glutton and a drunkard.' Then all the men of his town are to stone him to death. You must purge the evil from among you. All Israel will hear of it and be afraid."[47]

Yikes! What mom or dad would want to follow this commandment from the Torah? By implementing a variety of classical rabbinic legal interpretive strategies, the rabbis of the Mishnah whittle down the pool of people who could ever be convicted of being a "stubborn or rebellious son" so severely that it becomes utterly impossible for anyone to ever fall into this category. One Talmudic rabbi goes so far as to state that there never was anyone who was a "stubborn and rebellious son" and there never would be! Another rabbi asks what the purpose was of this entire passage being in the Torah if it would never actually apply to a real person, and the reply he receives from a fellow sage is that God put the text in the Torah only so that Jews could study it and be rewarded for their study.

Ben sorer u-moreh is a great example of how sometimes a religious tradition successfully mutes the potential harm of its texts of cruelty by means of traditionally approved methods of interpretation, and all without challenging the belief in the moral perfection or total Divine authorship of the core sacred text. But in too many instances, in Judaism and in other religions, sacred texts of cruelty go unreformed and continue to be used to teach false ideas about what God is like and what kinds of actions

47. Deut 21:18–21, *NIV.*

God wants us to take. Or, these texts lie dormant for centuries but are then pulled out by extremists who use them to rally followers around acts of violence.

Instead of accepting these sorts of interpretive somersaults that religions sometimes employ to tame some of their texts of cruelty, I believe there is a more honest and reliable approach to defanging these dangerous texts. It is, as I said earlier, for people to choose to be participants rather than followers of their religions—more specifically, for people to be *active participants in a religion's ongoing search for Truth, accepting that from the beginning, a religion has produced both true insights about God as well as spiritual errors, and that a religion's sacred texts are not perfect, but rather represent a record of that religion's imperfect but noble search for Truth.* By being this kind of participant, a person can draw from the wells of her religion's insights and genius, and simultaneously choose to be honest about the religion's spiritual and moral mistakes in order to learn from them.

***

I mentioned at the beginning of this chapter that when Jews gather on Shabbat, we chant the weekly Torah portion according to a specific musical system of cantillation called trope. There are different tropes for different Jewish holy days and for different books of the Hebrew Bible. Each trope musically conveys a different mood. Torah trope—at least most European varieties of it—is in a major key and has a mood that I can only describe as declarative and straightforward. The trope system that is used for chanting the Books of the Prophets, known as *haftarah* trope, is in a minor key and has a wistful and ancient feel.

Once a year, when Jews observe the holy day known as the Fast of the Ninth of Av (*Tisha B'Av* in Hebrew), we chant from the biblical book of Lamentations. The Ninth of Av was the date on the Hebrew calendar when the Babylonian empire destroyed the holy Temple in Jerusalem in 586 BCE. The Roman Empire repeated this horrific act of destruction in the year 70 CE on the same date. Other historical calamities happened to the Jewish people on this date as well. The tradition on Tisha B'Av is to chant Lamentations according to a special trope created just for this book. It is the most mournful sounding of all the tropes—a melody of grief and catastrophic sadness. It is the sound of people who are witnesses to destruction and are left asking why.

Taking a cue from the conversation that Rev. Taussig's congregants had with the synagogue community they had studied with, I would like to suggest an option based on an expansion of an idea proposed by the contemporary Jewish artist and teacher Rivka Walton: that synagogues call attention to the Torah's texts of cruelty by continuing to chant these texts as usual when they come up, but to chant them according to Lamentations trope, not the standard Torah trope.[48] As the Jewish philosopher Judith Plaskow wrote about Walton's suggestion, "Varying trope is a classic way of expressing feelings and values surrounding the material being read, and it has the advantage of calling community attention to morally difficult texts in the very process of reading."[49] Plaskow also suggests that discussion of how these texts have been, or are currently being, used to advance violence and cruelty could accompany the Torah chanting on these dates.[50] Synagogues could use these texts as opportunities to examine their values and take moral responsibility for the areas in which their religious tradition has done, and continues to do, damage—from the perspective that *all* religions do some good and do some damage. A potent ritual tool like the trope for Lamentations can publicly announce that something out of the ordinary is taking place during the usual Torah chanting on Shabbat. Lamentations trope can "testify against" the spiritual and moral errors of texts of cruelty in the Torah.

One of the early rabbis of the Mishnah wrote that a person shouldn't make a crown or a spade out of the Torah.[51] The idea is that a person shouldn't use the Torah as a means of self-aggrandizement (crown) or as a crass tool to make money (spade). I would like to add to this teaching a new saying: *Don't make a weapon out of the Torah.* Or any other sacred text. One of the most important religious lessons of all—that we not be blind followers of our prophets or sacred texts, and that we refuse to use our religions to cause harm—is also a lesson we can learn from Moses.

48. Plaskow, "Dealing with the Hard Stuff," 57.
49. Ibid.
50. Ibid.
51. This is a paraphrasing of part of *m. Avot* 4:7.

9

Rav Lach

Moses Experiences Life's Harsh Boundaries

WHILE THE JEWS WANDERED in the wilderness for forty years en route to the Promised Land, Moses committed a sin that resulted in God deciding that he would not be allowed to enter the Land of Israel along with the Hebrews.[1] This was a devastating loss for Moses. Near the end of his life, he tried in vain to persuade God to permit him to at least set foot in the Promised Land and take a brief tour of its different regions. Here's how Moses, addressing the Israelites, described his final plea to God on this matter:

> Then I pleaded with the Eternal at that time, saying: "O Eternal God, You have begun to show Your servant Your greatness and Your mighty hand, for what god is there in heaven or on earth who can do anything like Your works and Your mighty deeds? I pray, let me cross over and see the good land beyond the Jordan, those pleasant mountains, and Lebanon."
>
> But the Eternal was angry with me on your account, and would not listen to me. So the Eternal said to me: "*Rav Lach!* This is enough for you! Speak no more to Me of this matter. Go up to the top of Pisgah, and lift your eyes toward the west, the north,

1. Num 20.

the south, and the east; behold it with your eyes, for you shall not cross over this Jordan. But command Joshua, and encourage him and strengthen him; for he shall go over before this people, and he shall cause them to inherit the land which you will see."[2]

The ancient rabbis amplified Moses' heartbreak. Rabbi Jonathan Stein describes the midrash as follows, "Moses begs God for favor and forgiveness for his sins. He tells God that he has been held to a higher standard and prays 515 times for a reversal of the decree. Moses pleads with God to make him into an animal and let him at least touch the land, but God refuses. God then relents a little and allows Moses to view the Promised Land. Other midrashim also contain the same general theme."[3]

Once, after I gave a *d'var Torah* (a sermon based on the weekly Torah portion) on this passage from Deuteronomy, my mom asked me why I thought God didn't allow Moses to set even one foot in the Promised Land. She just couldn't get her mind around the harshness of not allowing this great man his dying wish; this man, who—whatever his mistakes might have been—had struggled so intensely for over forty years on behalf of God and the Jewish people. It was then I had a thought (that others may have had before me) . . .

Maybe this whole passage isn't really about what Moses deserved or didn't deserve. Maybe what the Torah is describing here is just one of those hard-edged boundaries of life. Maybe the entire story of Moses' life and death, with its surprising opportunities for greatness and its terrible disappointments, is meant to teach us about one of the ultimate truths about the human condition. We get some opportunities to do meaningful and remarkable things in our lives (not necessarily the things we expect), and then there are some things we want so very badly that we just never get to do. Maybe what we can learn from Moses' life is that even someone who gets to do the most extraordinary things—great things that he never dreamed as a younger person he'd ever have anything to do with—*even* such a person experiences the hard-edged boundaries of life and death like the rest of us.

2. Deut 3:23–28, *NIV* (Hebrew insertion and changes to the NIV English translation mine).

3. Stein, "The Divine Kiss." "Midrashim" is the Hebrew plural for the singular, "midrash."

In commenting on this part of Torah, Rabbi Michael Signer writes, "A modern proverb that asserts that expectations are planned disappointments may be most appropriate to describe the sad moment in Moses' life when he realizes that there will be no more pleading. He must simply accept the fact that he will not complete the task according to his own vision. Our own need to control our fate and have the validation of the complete fulfillment of our labors may find resonance in the exchange between Moses and God."[4]

The flip side of life's *Rav Lach /"This is enough for you!"* moments is that sometimes life also presents us with unexpected opportunities for higher meaning. Remember, after Moses fled Egypt following his killing of the Egyptian overseer, he went on to build an entirely new life as a shepherd of Jethro's flocks in Midian. He settles in to this life, becomes married with kids, and finds some measure of peace and stability, maybe even happiness.

At this point, Moses already had a remarkable life. How many people start out life amongst royalty in palaces and complete it amongst sheep in rugged desert terrain? Whatever Moses may have wanted in life by the time he'd been a husband, father, and son-in-law in Midian for many years—and however he had come to terms with all that he'd lost in Egypt—it all was about to change in ways he could never have imagined.

When God spoke to him from the burning bush at Mount Sinai, life suddenly launched Moses on a new trajectory, and the opportunities for creating higher meaning in his life shifted without warning. Harsh disappointments and unexpected opportunities for higher meaning—that's what life gave Moses, and that's what life gives most of us.

The year I had that conversation with my mom, Moses had caused me to think a lot about the unexpected opportunities for meaning and the terrible disappointments in my life. For it was earlier that year that my wife, Melissa, and I had done something we never knew we would do for most of the time we'd known each other. After years of battling infertility, and after carefully exploring all our adoption alternatives, we ended up adopting two older children from our state's foster care system. This brought the unexpected into our lives in so many ways. Just to name one of many surprises: with my love for Hebrew names, I certainly didn't think I would end up with a son named Hunter. Or a daughter named Clarice.

4. Signer, "Visions, Conclusions, and Beginnings."

Rebecca and David, Rachel and Nathan—that was what I had imagined. The Universe, God, Life, Fate, or Something had other ideas.

Also, for my entire adult life, I had thought that I would create the greatest meaning in my life through my work. And yet the biggest opportunity of my entire life for living out higher meaning came to me in the form of two children who were born three thousand miles away from me, without my knowledge, while I was studying for the rabbinate in Philadelphia. The moment Clarice and Hunter became a part of our lives was the moment God called Melissa and me away, by name, from our other preoccupations, just like God called Moses away from tending the sheep near Mount Sinai. Hunter and Clarice were presented to us as a remarkable opportunity to change the whole course of our lives, and like Moses at the burning bush, we chose to say, *Hineini*—"here I am"—and step into the unknown.

Like so many people, and like Moses, the great opportunities for higher meaning in my spouse's and my life came from unanticipated places and have taken us into new territory. We've given ourselves over to the journey and we're thankful to God for it. And yet, like Moses and everyone else, we've also experienced the harsh, hard edges of life. We desperately wanted to have biological children. God said, "No, you can't go into that land." Hundreds of times I said the same prayer that so many of our biblical ancestors offered with successful outcomes: "Please, God, let us conceive." After the clock ticked away our hope, God's silence felt to me like God's final refusal to Moses' plea to enter the Promised Land: "*Rav Lach!* This is enough for you! Speak no more to Me of this matter."

A hard-edged boundary. A disappointment with so many layered dimensions of loss. I lost my father when I was eighteen. I don't really look much like him. He had red hair and green eyes. I have brown hair and brown eyes. I was his only child. One of the only genetic legacies he left me that I can see with my own eyes is a sprinkling of red whiskers in my beard. I consoled myself for years with the thought that I would pass on some of him through my kids—my biological kids carrying his precious genes. Maybe one of my children would have red hair. Please, God? *Rav lach.* You will not enter that land. Others will cross that river and revel in it. Not you. Speak to Me no more of this matter.

The bottom line is that our individual stories are embedded in a larger story that has its own unpredictable flow. Sometimes we can influence that flow, but when life takes a twist that presents us with a harsh boundary, we're wise to yield. It's the same with the unexpected opportunities for higher meaning that life presents us. Sometimes these opportunities are the ones we work for and plan for. But sometimes they come out of the blue and give us the option of making an unexpected journey out of our lives. Moses' remarkable life of unanticipated greatness and devastating disappointment encourages us to make the most of the opportunities life gives us to be agents of higher purpose, and to reconcile ourselves to the borders and edges that life presents us all.

10

"Moses"

SINCE 1985 A GROUP of Christian Bible scholars have worked on what has been known as the Jesus Seminar. Their Web site states, "the Seminar was organized to discover and report a scholarly consensus on the historical authenticity of the sayings . . . and events . . . attributed to Jesus in the gospels."[1] Even though their work involves questioning the historical accuracy of how the New Testament presents Jesus, many of the Jesus Seminar professors are also Christian pastors committed to a living Christian faith. By closely analyzing the New Testament texts and reviewing other available historical information, these scholars have sought to develop theories about who the actual, historical Jesus may have been, and which sayings and actions attributed to him are most likely to be authentic. In part, what they seek to do is better understand how their religion evolved in its first two centuries of being. They want to better understand the various early Christian groups that produced the different Gospels, for instance, and how each of them may have shaped or added to the teachings attributed to Jesus over the years.

It's important to bear in mind that in the ancient world the common practice was for disciples of a great master to add to his (or occasionally, her) sayings and teachings. When faithful disciples would add to their master's sayings, they would often attribute the new sayings to him, out of respect and loyalty to the school of thought that he had founded. Disciples

1. Online at: http://www.westarinstitute.org/Seminars/seminars.html.

and students were not eager to claim personal authorship of new ideas for themselves, nor did they have the need modern Westerners often have for historical accuracy. When rival groups of disciples of the same master would interpret the master's life and teachings differently, they would be sure to develop additional sayings in his name that reflected their varying ideological perspectives. In this way a master's teachings would sometimes develop over time along different ideological lines, in some cases evolving beyond what the master himself would have condoned or even imagined.

This was a practice that was so normal that it was not noteworthy in the ancient world. (Omid Safi, an Islamic studies professor, commenting about similar processes that have played out in Islam, writes: "There might have been one historical Muhammad, but there have been many memories of Muhammad."[2]) In Jewish tradition, scholars see the same pattern having played out among the early rabbis. There are many teachings and sayings attributed in the Talmud to great sages like Hillel or Rabbi Akiva, for example. Both men had many disciples and developed popular schools of thought. It is likely that over time, sayings accrued to them that they never actually uttered.

Sometimes different groups within a developing religious tradition would join together to consolidate and canonize an official version of their sacred texts. This usually involved discussion and compromise, as the different groups would want their own texts and traditions included in the canon. In the ancient Middle East, the canonizers of sacred texts were not operating within the framework of modern Western writing, and therefore they were quite comfortable putting multiple and even contradictory written traditions alongside each other as part of the finalized sacred canon. The canonizers of the New Testament, like the redactors of the Torah that I discussed in chapter 6, were not threatened by presenting their contemporary readers with a Bible designed as a composite text that includes multiple accounts of the same story, complete with contradictions and logical or narrative conflicts. This is why there are four Gospels in the New Testament, not just one. The New Testament even presents two Gospels that have conflicting genealogies of Jesus' ancestry.[3]

As the scholars involved in the Jesus Seminar have continued their work, they have offered a new way of looking at Jesus as he is presented in

2. Safi, *Memories of Muhammad*, 43.
3. The Gospels of Matthew and Luke.

103

the New Testament. They see the Jesus who emerges from the totality of their canonical sacred texts as a literary composite figure, a combination of some of his own authentic teachings as well as the varying and sometimes conflicting teachings of others who came after him. Some of these scholars have even started writing about the difference between "Jesus" and Jesus. "Jesus" is the composite literary character we find when we take the entire New Testament as a whole that is made up of many component parts: different writings from different communities with different agendas, writings that were joined together by editors and canonizers. Jesus— without quotes—is the historical person who lived, taught, inspired large numbers of people, and died about two thousand years ago in Roman occupied Judea.

Needless to say, the written use of "Jesus" as a way of making a distinction that is important to the Jesus Seminar scholars was bound to upset some Christian religious traditionalists. One of the most common criticisms of the Jesus Seminar from some Christian conservatives is that their entire endeavor is heresy. Once they deconstruct traditional Christian belief to the point that Jesus becomes "Jesus," the critics argue, they've left the fold. Many liberal Christians, on the other hand, disagree, and don't see a threat to their tradition through this kind of historical inquiry.

In rabbinical school we were required to take a course on Christianity taught by a local Methodist minister—the same one I discussed in chapter 8—who is also a Jesus Seminar scholar. Rev. Dr. Hal Taussig shared how the research he has done into who the historical Jesus might have been has deepened his appreciation for the best aspects of his religion. In addition to the interest he expressed in discovering which sayings and teachings are most likely to have been authentic to the historical Jesus, Dr. Taussig also has found great value in identifying the sayings that were most likely attributed to Jesus by others during the decades following his death. This information reveals insight into how spiritual life developed in early Christian communities under different circumstances. What Dr. Taussig modeled was a way of relating to one's own religion with an attitude of excitement and curiosity about what kinds of truth and beauty one might see if one is willing to look behind the curtain of the myth, letting go of dogma and approaching the past with a sense of curiosity and adventure.[4]

4. I have paraphrased things I learned from Dr. Taussig in the Christianity course I took while in rabbinical school at the Reconstructionist Rabbinical College.

It's in this same spirit that I have chosen to write this last chapter not on Moses, but rather on "Moses."

***

Because Jesus' lifetime was at least twelve hundred years closer to our time than Moses'; because the New Testament includes four distinct Gospels and many other writings about Jesus' teachings and beliefs; and because there are also several known Gospels that were not canonized into the Christian Bible, there is enough written, archeological, and historical material available to scholars to do fruitful investigative work on the question of what the historical Jesus may have actually preached, done, and taught. In the case of Moses, however, it's harder to make this kind of inquiry. With Moses we're talking about events purported to have happened approximately thirty-three hundred to thirty-five hundred years ago. The New Testament was canonized within only 350 years of the life of Jesus, and much of it was written within a century of his death. The Torah on the other hand, according to most Bible scholars, didn't come into its final redacted form until about seven hundred or more years after when Moses likely lived. And the rest of the Hebrew Bible, including its accounts of Moses, took several more centuries to come together.

The Jesus Seminar scholars are also fortunate to be able to draw upon many available ancient writings about Jesus from non-Christian sources, such as the early rabbis, the Romans, and others. All of these sources are influenced by the agendas and polemics of their authors, to be sure, but nevertheless they are valuable for historical research. By contrast, there aren't any surviving documents about Moses from non-Israelite sources close to the time of his life. One of the great disappointments of Middle Eastern archeology has been the utter lack of any ancient Egyptian accounts of Hebrew slavery or of Moses, their liberator.

Moses' great antiquity makes him a very distant mythical figure, and the oldest account of him we have is the Torah's complex and composite presentation of him. Still, like the historical Jesus scholars, I can't help but wonder two things: 1) Who was the historical Moses, and 2) what valuable things can we learn by studying the elements that make up "Moses" as he has been presented by the Torah, by Jewish tradition as it evolved over the centuries, and by other religions that have added their own layerings to this remarkable composite figure?

Truth be told, I'm actually more interested in the second question than the first. Barring some amazing archeological discoveries in the future, the historical Moses will probably always remain beyond our reach. Academic Bible scholars debate the question of whether there was an historical Moses, and among those who believe there was, opinions about who he was and what he did vary. A few have even suggested that Moses was actually an Egyptian noble who followed the monotheistic beliefs of a Pharaoh whose short reign had preceded the dynasty that witnessed the Hebrew slaves' escape, though this theory is not believed by many in the field.[5] In the end, unless we choose to believe a traditional religious narrative about Moses, we are left with a mystery as to whether or not he existed, and if he did, who he was and what he might actually have said and done. And without the kinds of corroborating materials that have helped to confirm the historical existence of other giant religious personalities, like Jesus and Muhammad, we are left with only plausible theories and educated speculation.

For me, what the historical Moses may have been like is not so important. The person found in the Jewish sacred literature that I have studied, learned from, and at times wrestled with as part of my life as a thoughtful and committed Jew is "Moses," not Moses, and I'm comfortable with that. Let's look at how "Moses" has evolved over the centuries.

First, let's explore what we can learn by trying to tease apart some of the layers of the literary composite figure of "Moses" presented to us in the Torah. According to the Documentary Hypothesis developed by academic biblical scholarship, roughly 2,500 years ago the redactors of the Torah wove together different traditions about Moses that came largely from four major scribal schools, which academics named J, E, P, and D. Scholars such as Moshe Greenberg also argue that in addition to these four sources, there was probably a core legal tradition that Moses actually presented to the ancient Hebrews. Over the centuries, however, the Israelites developed additional laws and ascribed them to Moses, and these laws also became part of the final Torah text.[6]

If the Documentary Hypothesis is more or less on target, the "Moses" of Torah is a composite figure who binds together different legal codes,

---

5. Sigmund Freud helped popularize this thesis with a book he wrote in the 1930s, *Moses and Monotheism*.

6. Greenberg, "Moses," 386.

stories, leadership roles, and personality traits. Although much has been written about the writing styles as well as the spiritual, legal, and political priorities of J, E, P, and D, there is no scholarly consensus on exactly how to divide up the different source materials of the Torah's accounts of Moses. Moses' enormity as a character in the Torah, the sophistication of the editing, as well as the number of unknowns about the development of these different textual sources combine to thwart efforts at scholarly consensus.

For example, take the Torah's lengthy telling of the geographic movement of Moses and the Israelites once they escape Egypt and begin their forty-year journey in the wilderness. This story begins in the book of Exodus and ends in Deuteronomy. From a simple narrative standpoint, it's hard to follow precisely where the Israelites are throughout the story and what the chronological order of the episodes is. Also, sometimes the Torah's wilderness narrative presents inconsistencies, or offers multiple tellings of similar episodes. Scholars think that one reason for these narrative curiosities is that, in this part of the Torah, multiple traditions of story and lawgiving have been woven together with an editorial emphasis on preserving and combining various story traditions.

I won't present a lengthy overview here of the different ways that J, E, P, and D each give us a "Moses" whom the redactors ultimately merged together into the "Moses" we know in Torah. That would be an entire book in and of itself, and several other Bible scholars have already written that book. Rather, I'll limit myself to mentioning two examples of what we discover when we separate the literary strands of the Torah's "Moses," and I'll talk about why it's worthwhile for us to study the source texts independently alongside the Torah's final version.

First example: Exodus 14—the splitting of the Sea of Reeds. Many Bible scholars see two story traditions about the miracle at the sea woven together, along with some other materials, to form a composite, single telling of this crucial episode. One of the major literary sources, P, tells the tale by using the images we're most familiar with. Moses raises his rod and the sea splits down the middle. The Israelites march between two standing walls of water, and when the Egyptian charioteers give chase, the walls of the sea collapse upon them. Another source, J, tells a different story: during the night a powerful low tide combined with a strong wind pushes back the sea and allows the Hebrews to go forward on shoreland that had previously been underwater. (There are no walls of water surrounding the slaves as they go forward.) God's protective pillar of cloud delays the Egyptian pursuit, but when the Pharaoh's warriors finally do give chase, the wind changes direction and the tide comes back more fiercely and quickly than they were expecting. They turn their chariots around to head back, but it's too late, and they are trapped in the returning salty waters.[7]

The final edited version of the story we read in Exodus 14 emphasizes P's imagery while using J's to support the tale. The narrative shifts between P, J, and other materials, creating a final version that flows well enough as a single narrative for us to follow along, but that has just enough jumping around from one vantage point to another to heighten the sense of chaos in the story. This is part of the literary craftsmanship of the redactors.

Given that the redactors' final version of this story is so wonderfully composed, what's to be gained by studying its different literary source texts? Well, to offer just one response: studying the P and J strands of this story opens up important questions about the character of Moses in this climactic moment. Moses' actions and words in P and J present us with different snapshots of his leadership in a situation of terrible peril.

In P, when the Hebrews are crying out in prayer to be rescued, God tells Moses not to just stand helplessly among them, but to raise up his rod before them so that the sea can part. *Snap out of your shock, Moses, and do something!* Moses' leadership response to the crisis is to take bold and visible action. He raises his rod and the miracle happens.

In J, however, when the Hebrews panic, Moses uses a different approach, speaking these words to the people: "Don't be afraid. Stand still and watch the divine salvation that God will do for you today."[8] Moses doesn't raise his rod, and the sea doesn't split. He does precisely the opposite of what he did in the P account—he purposely just stands there amidst the terrifying clamor. *Be still and pay attention* is his Zen-like message. *Trust.* A strong east wind blows back the waters and makes a way forward for the Hebrews, while the Egyptians' view of things is obscured by God's pillar of cloud.

By teasing apart these two strands of the Torah's composite telling of the redemption at the sea, we see two possible models of leadership in a moment of great danger. Two different "Moseses." If we didn't go through

7. Gottwald, *The Hebrew Bible*, 198–99.
8. Exod 14:13. Translation mine.

this exercise, we would miss the opportunity to explore what we can learn from these two different examples of leadership in a crisis. Studying the P and J strands of the story raises new questions, such as: When people are in a panic, when is one leadership tactic more effective than another? When does the situation call for a proactive gesture (P) or an unflappable and trusting posture (J)? This is the value in breaking down the literary sources of the Torah's accounts of Moses—each strand has its own conversations to spark and teachings to offer.

When we study the combined, finalized Torah story that the redactors bound together in Exodus 14, we get yet another "Moses" to discuss. The redactors' "Moses" is a leader who moves back and forth between the more active, visible leadership of P and the more trusting, quiet-in-the-face-of-danger approach of J, perhaps offering the lesson that a truly effective leader needs to be nimble and flexibly responsive to different people's needs in a crisis.

For a second example of what we can learn when we separate biblical literary strands that make up a single episode in the text, let's turn to another part of the Torah. Some Bible scholars believe that the Torah has artfully combined two different traditions about the location of where the Israelites had their main revelatory encounter with God in the wilderness. Most of us are familiar with the Torah's accounts of God giving the Israelites the commandments amidst thunder and lightning at Mount Sinai, but the Torah also describes divine laws being presented to the Israelites in another location: the wilderness oasis of Kadesh, where the Israelites encamped for some time during their forty years of wandering.

Norman K. Gottwald writes that two different traditions about where the people received the Law have been preserved in the Torah, though the redactors chose to emphasize the Sinai encounter.[9] One of the reasons he presents this theory is based on some striking storytelling parallels that he observes in the Torah's presentation of the Israelites' experiences at Mount Sinai and Kadesh.[10]

Why would there be a Sinai and a Kadesh tradition about the Israelites' experience of receiving God's laws? One theory suggests that the Israelites were a people that were made up of two different groups that joined together and merged their religious traditions, laws, and stories.

9. Gottwald, *The Hebrew Bible*, 199–200.
10. Ibid., 200.

One group went through slavery in Egypt and the exodus. When they left Egypt they went to Mount Sinai and received the Law, and then later made their way to Kadesh. The other group, however, was never enslaved, but rather had lived at Kadesh for some time.[11] They had traditions of having encountered their deity and received their laws at Kadesh. Sometime after meeting up at Kadesh, the two groups eventually merged. According to some versions of this theory, the historical Moses was the great leader of the group that left Egypt, and ultimately he became incorporated into the Kadesh group's mythic traditions as their lawgiver too. There's no way to prove or disprove this theory, of course. It's perfectly possible that there weren't two different groups that merged at Kadesh, or that the Israelite people formed out of some other kind of merging of groups.

But by taking the time to consider the possibility that there was a "Slaves in Egypt" group and a "Kadesh" group, we open up to new possibilities about who Moses may have been and how the early Israelite religion evolved in its first stages. Maybe in addition to being a liberator, a legislator, a prophet of God, and a military leader, we should add to Moses' leadership roles that he was a *negotiator* between tribal peoples. Maybe it was Moses who worked tirelessly so that these two groups could connect their fates, interweaving their theologies, religious stories, laws, and practices.

Furthermore, if Moses led a group of Hebrew slaves out of Egypt and took them to the lush oasis of Kadesh, maybe Moses *didn't* fail to lead the people into the Promised Land after all! Elias Auerbach, in advocating this theory, writes:

> At the [time of the] Exodus, the goal of the Israelites was not Canaan at all. They stayed for decades in the wilderness, because their goal . . . was to settle down for a long time. This goal, which emerges from all the old accounts, was the oasis of Kadesh . . . Kadesh is the largest oasis of the Sinai Peninsula, irrigated by several powerful springs. It stretches out several miles in breadth and about fifteen miles in length, covering an area of some sixty square miles and thereby offering space and sustenance to a population of several thousand people. The scanty reports we have from travelers agree that in the burning wilderness the oasis appears like a paradise. Murmuring brooks, rich vegetation of grass, trees and shrubs and flowers, birds and insects conjure up a truly fairylike

11. Ibid., 201.

picture to the traveler who is arriving from the desert. For the poor
Bedouin who knows hardly anything except severe privations, this
too is "a land flowing with milk and honey."[12]

According to this theory, over some time the confederation of the
two groups solidified, and they developed a new goal: conquest of the
relatively fertile and more spacious land of Canaan. Canaan would replace
Kadesh in this emerging people's mythic story as the Promised Land.
Now, of course, this could all be wrong. But by weighing the evidence for
these kinds of scenarios, and by looking at the likely strands and layers of
the Torah's composite text, we gain alternative impressions of "Moses" and
new insights into who he might have been—insights that are not offered
to us if we limit ourselves to only those readings of the Torah that are approved by religious doctrine.

***

"Moses received the Torah at Mount Sinai, and he transmitted it to Joshua; and Joshua to the elders; and the elders to the
prophets; and the prophets transmitted it to the men of the Great
Assembly"—MISHNAH AVOT 1:1A[13]

After the Roman decimation of ancient Israelite civilization two thousand
years ago, Jewish scholars and teachers known as rabbis worked hard to
pick up the broken pieces of their religion and reconstruct it into a form
that could survive the new conditions of exile and political disempow-
erment. The rabbis built on traditions they had been developing for at
least the last two centuries before the Roman exile. While the Temple still
stood in Jerusalem, the earliest of these rabbis represented a source of religious authority that was both complementary to and competitive with the
Temple priesthood. The relationship between the Temple priests and the
rabbis during the last decades that the Temple stood was complex and at
times quite hostile. Once the Temple was in ruins and the priests had lost
the institution in which they had played their ritual and religious roles,
the rabbis stepped into the vacuum and began a multi-century effort to
rebuild Israelite religion as a portable tradition that could function for

12. Auerbach, *Moses*, 66–67.
13. Translation mine.

newly exiled Jewish communities flung across the stretches of the Roman empire.

At the center of the rabbinic enterprise was an emphasis on the Torah and the interpretations of it that rabbis had been developing in their academies for some time. Their method of transmitting these interpretations was oral, and they came to call the entire body of rabbinic interpretive teaching the "Oral Torah." (They also coined the term "the Written Torah" to refer to the Five Books of Moses, Genesis through Deuteronomy.) Eventually, the Oral Torah became so voluminous that about two hundred years after the Roman destruction, a powerful rabbi, Judah the Prince, had a compilation of these teachings written down and disseminated throughout the Jewish world. This book is called the Mishnah. With the arrival of the Mishnah, the Oral Torah ironically became written down.

The text quoted above (m. Avot 1:1) is one of the most important teachings in the Oral Torah, because it makes the claim that the rabbis are the continuous and authentic heirs to and interpreters of the Written Torah that Moses received from God atop Mount Sinai. What m. Avot 1:1 is saying is that Moses passed on the Torah he received from God, and that others continued to pass it on through a specific chain, ultimately leading to a group called the Men of the Great Assembly. The rabbis understood these men to be the forerunners of themselves.

The rabbis went a step further with their claim to the sole mantle of legitimate Jewish religious authority. They asserted that their Oral Torah also was revealed by God to Moses at Mount Sinai along with the Written Torah. Moses, they claimed, then transmitted these rabbinic interpretations and additions to the Written Torah to Joshua, and then Joshua passed them on down through the chain.

This rabbinic theology—that there were actually *two* Torahs that were given to Moses at Mount Sinai, one written and one oral, and that both were taught and transmitted by Moses himself—is the most important new layer of mythologizing that the rabbinic tradition added to the evolving composite figure of "Moses." They recast Moses as a teacher of rabbinic legal interpretations who was knowledgable of the Oral Torah. Bear in mind that the Oral Torah includes many legal debates and disagreements among rabbis who lived many centuries after Moses, and that it is *all of this* that Moses is somehow described as having received from

God at Mount Sinai.[14] The rabbis not only recast Moses as the father of the rabbinic interpretive tradition, they took to referring to him as "Moses our rabbi," *Moshe rabbeinu* in Hebrew. Moses, who never heard of such a thing as a rabbi, becomes a rabbi himself in this rabbinic reenvisioning of who and what he was. In Moses the rabbis saw something of themselves.

***

Fast forward eight hundred years or so to about the year 1190 CE, and we find the Jewish people continuing to live in communities spread out all over the lands that at one time had been part of the Roman Empire. Medieval Jews lived either under European Christian or North African/ Middle Eastern Islamic authorities. The majority of the world's Jews had long since accepted rabbinic authority, though a large and committed minority of Jews followed a non-rabbinic approach to Judaism known as Karaism (see chapter 5 for more on the Karaites).

In parts of the Islamic world, Jewish intellectual life was flourishing. Philosophy and science were popular among the prominent thinkers and writers in the Muslim and Jewish world. As discussed in chapter 5, the most influential of the Jewish philosopher-rabbis of this era was Maimonides, also known as the Rambam or Moses ben Maimon. Born in Muslim-ruled Spain, Maimonides experienced a painful period in Muslim-Jewish relations when a fundamentalist Islamic sect seized power in Spain and, in an act of intolerance uncharacteristic of their Muslim predecessors, expelled the Jews from the region where Maimonides lived.

Moses ben Maimon relocated to Fustat, near Cairo in the cosmopolitan and tolerant Muslim community of Egypt. There he worked as a physician to the Islamic elite, while finding time to write extensively. One of his life's greatest achievements was the writing of a philosophical discussion of the "correct" understanding of Torah, *The Guide for the Perplexed*. With the *Guide*, Maimonides sought to harmonize the teachings of Torah with the beliefs of the philosophy and science of his times.

14. Some rabbis argue that what God transmitted to Moses at Mount Sinai as the Oral Torah was not the actual content of all the interpretations, additions, debates, and comments that later rabbis would make, but rather the *methodology* of rabbinic interpretation, or even just the holy *spark of inspiration* leading to correct interpretations of the Written Torah. Others understood the tradition of the dual revelation of Written and Oral Torah to Moses more literally.

The dominant medieval philosophy was based on the ideas of Plato and Aristotle, whose writings had been preserved by Islamic civilization. This philosophy posited the idea that God is a disembodied, unified source of energy, radiating out in all directions, and that God's overflowing energy created the entire universe. This kind of God is unknowable to humans—our intellect simply can't grasp It.

In the *Guide,* Maimonides makes the case that every place in the Torah that refers to God anthropomorphically is actually metaphorical, and that a person of an advanced intellectual and moral capacity should realize this. When the Torah says that God "walked," "spoke," or "stretched out His arm," its sole intent is to function as a teaching text that can help people at all stages of intellectual and moral development advance to the next level. These images of a God with a human body are intended for children and simpletons, Maimonides wrote, but those who are more advanced will understand that all this language is nonliteral and in fact includes encoded teachings that mean something else. What sorts of encoded teachings? Well, according to Maimonides, often the encoded teachings in these passages are the Torah's allegorical version of the tenets of Greek philosophy.[15]

The philosophy that Maimonides regarded as a source of truth alongside Torah shaped his understanding of who Moses was. Moses was, for Maimonides, first and foremost a prophet—*the* prophet/philosopher par excellence. The difficulty Maimonides faced was that the Torah and the rest of the Hebrew Bible frequently depict God *speaking* to the prophets, and, of course, the God Maimonides believed in didn't have a mouth and certainly didn't talk. What Maimonides' God did do, however, was emanate energy in the way that Plato had described, kind of like a cosmic radio transmitter emitting radio waves.[16] In the *Guide,* Maimonides depicts the Hebrew prophets as individuals who were so excellent in their morality and intelligence that their own intellects became attuned to the ever-present Divine energy that flows uninterrupted throughout the cos-

15. Interestingly, Maimonides was not the first Jewish scholar to promote the idea that the Torah uses allegory and symbolism to teach central philosophical ideas valued by the ancient Greeks. About a thousand years earlier, Philo of Alexandria, a Hellenized Jew living in Egypt, wrote treatises making similar claims. Philo's "Moses," like Maimonides's "Moses," is a master of Greek philosophy's theological ideas.

16. I learned this metaphor in a class at the Reconstructionist Rabbinical College taught by Dr. Jacob Staub.

mos. Maimonides describes Moses as the human being whose "antenna," if you will, was better attuned to the energy transmissions of God than any person who ever lived or ever would live, and that is why he became the greatest of all the prophets.

So, Maimonides taught, God never actually *said* anything to Moses. Instead of taking all of the Torah's dialogues and even arguments between God and Moses literally, what actually happened, according to Maimonides, was that in each of those scenes Moses' prophetic skills allowed him to "tune in" to the Divine energy. This led Moses to receive an internal understanding of God's truth and God's will, and Moses then relayed this knowledge in the form of teachings that the Israelites could comprehend.

In Maimonides' view of things, we are not meant to take literally the traditional Jewish belief that God verbally dictated, word by word, the Torah to Moses, who faithfully wrote it down atop Mount Sinai. Rather, Maimonides gives us a Moses who went into deep prophetic meditation upon the mountain, and, as a result of acutely "tuning in" to the Divine energy flow, wrote the Torah.[17] Maimonides goes further to state that Moses understood that the average Jew wouldn't be able to grasp the esoteric truths of the Divine message, and so Moses deliberately wrote the Torah as a document designed to enable people to move, step by step, closer to the truth by studying it and advancing from one intellectual and moral level to the next. Maimonides argued that Moses sometimes chose to describe God in anthropomorphic terms for the purpose of teaching kids and people of poor intellectual capacities the basics of the moral life. The same Torah invites the growing and maturing student to begin to see through the ruse of the anthropomorphisms and discover the more subtle truths embedded in the Torah—truths that are understood when the Torah is seen as making analogies and offering hints and clues to more sophisticated meaning.[18]

Maimonides was the most prominent of many rabbis of his era who reconceived of God and of Moses in the light of the philosophy and sci-

17. Again, I credit Dr. Jacob Staub for the classes I took with him in which I learned many of the metaphors I've used in discussing Maimonides.

18. In chapter 32 of the *Guide* Maimonides actually uses the phrase "gracious ruse" to describe the Torah's use of anthropomorphic and other metaphorical language as an educational stepping-stone to help people at simpler stages of intellectual and spiritual maturity learn elementary lessons about God.

ence of the times. The medieval Jewish philosophers added yet another layer onto the composite figure of "Moses." They recast him as a neo-Platonic philosopher/prophet. In their view, Moses was someone who understood the truths of Greek philosophy, and therefore *Torah* and not the ancient Greeks deserved the credit for first presenting the world with great Hellenistic philosophical insights! And if Moses was a philosopher-rabbi, then Maimonides and his like-minded rabbinic colleagues were simply continuing the work that Moses himself had done. Once again, we have the Jews of a given period of history looking at Moses and seeing something of themselves.

We've now examined how the redactors of the Torah, the early rabbis, and the medieval Jewish philosophers each shaped and added layers of myth to the figure of Moses. What we see is a tendency of Jews to retroject their most powerful innovations in Jewish religious thought onto the figure of Moses. "Moses" has been a shape-shifter and an inspiration for one Jewish generation to the next. And this shouldn't surprise us, because it's a pattern we see in other religious traditions too. As Omid Safi writes, "we always remember and imagine the holy ones of the past partially through our own present lenses."[19]

In the next section of this chapter, we turn our attention to the way non-Jewish traditions have added their own layers of new mythology onto the composite figure of "Moses."

***

Christian tradition developed its own "Moses" as well. In the Gospel of Matthew, chapter 17, we find the following scene:

> After six days Jesus took with him Peter, James and John the brother of James, and led them up a high mountain by themselves. There he was transfigured before them. His face shone like the sun, and his clothes became as white as the light. Just then there appeared before them Moses and Elijah, talking with Jesus.
> Peter said to Jesus, "Lord, it is good for us to be here. If you wish, I will put up three shelters—one for you, one for Moses and one for Elijah."

19. Safi, *Memories of Muhammad*, 22.

> While he was still speaking, a bright cloud enveloped them,
> and a voice from the cloud said, "This is my Son, whom I love;
> with him I am well pleased. Listen to him!"
>
> When the disciples heard this, they fell face down to the
> ground, terrified. But Jesus came and touched them. "Get up,"
> he said. "Don't be afraid." When they looked up, they saw no one
> except Jesus.[20]

In this scene, known as the Transfiguration, Moses returns from the
dead and his presence with Jesus establishes Christianity as the sole legitimate heir to Israelite religion. The role the early Christians gave to Moses
in this passage as a validator of their religious beliefs is similar to the role
the early rabbis gave to Moses in the passage from the Mishnah we examined above. Moses suddenly appears in a new mythic story in both cases.
Here he stands with Jesus in counsel. For the rabbis, he received their
Oral Torah along with the Written Torah atop Mount Sinai. In both cases,
we're being told a new story that we didn't know before about something
important that happened in the life of Moses.

There are two other traditions in the Gospel of Matthew that involve
Moses directly. First, in the scene above, Jesus' face changes, shining like
the sun after his experience with God, Moses, and Elijah. This echoes
Exodus 34, which describes how Moses' face became radiant with light
after he returned from Mount Sinai with the second set of the tablets of
the Law. Moses had to wear a veil when addressing the people from this
point on, because the shining light from his face overwhelmed them. So a
symbol of Moses' unique and special designation by God is connected to
Jesus in this scene.

Second, chapter 2 of Matthew tells the tale of King Herod's attempt
to kill the baby Jesus. Having learned via an astrological sign and from
existing Hebrew prophecy that the "king of the Jews" had just been born
in Bethlehem, Herod gives an order to kill all the baby boys born in
Bethlehem. God's angel forewarns Joseph, who dispatches Mary and baby
Jesus to Egypt for safety. They stay there until Herod's death, and then
return to Judea, this time to Nazareth. This vignette's parallels and references to the perils faced by baby Moses in the book of Exodus are clear.
In Matthew, Moses' life takes on a new layer of significance—it prefigures
Jesus' life, even in its infancy.

20. Matt 17:1–8, *NIV.*

"Moses" for Christianity is a figure who towers over the mythic landscape up until the arrival of Jesus. He appears in the New Testament to validate the understanding that early followers of Jesus had that they were taking a religious path that was the true continuation of the religion of ancient Israel. For the many Jews who formed a large part of this following, an endorsement of their beliefs by Moses himself meant a great deal. As the centuries passed and Christianity developed as a religion distinct from Judaism, the Transfiguration came to be interpreted by many in the church as a scene in which Moses validates the truth of Christianity and the falseness of rabbinic Judaism. Where the rabbis found a fellow rabbi in Moses, the church found a prophet who returned from the dead to authenticate Jesus' place as God's son.

Roughly three centuries after the canonization of the New Testament, the earliest Muslims disseminated the Qur'an, the central sacred text of Islam. The Qur'an adds yet another layering onto "Moses." The Qur'an tells much of the same story as the Torah does about Moses, who is known in Arabic as the prophet Musa. Still, there are some prominent differences.

In the Qur'an, baby Moses is rescued from the Nile and then adopted jointly by the Pharaoh and his wife, Asiyah, whereas in Torah it is the Pharaoh's daughter who takes the basket carrying the Hebrew infant from the river.[21] The Qur'an also places the figure of Haman at Pharaoh's side as a wicked adviser. Jewish tradition knows Haman as the wicked adviser to the Persian king Achashverosh, in the biblical book of Esther. There are other differences involving basic story elements as well. For example, in the Qur'an, at one point Moses takes a journey with a wise and mysterious stranger in which he sees the stranger do several things that appear to be cruel and wicked on the surface, but these disturbing actions are ultimately revealed to have been righteous once Moses is made aware of the larger context.[22]

One significant Qur'anic story about Moses takes a key incident in Moses' life and offers a fascinating and different telling than the one found in the Torah. It gives us an example of how a later religious tradition can rework a known story for the purpose of emphasizing a particular moral teaching. In Exodus 2, Moses sees an Egyptian taskmaster brutalizing a Hebrew slave, and he deliberately strikes the man, killing him (the Torah

21. Sura 28.
22. Sura 18.

says that he looked around first to see if anyone was watching before he assaulted the Egyptian).[23] The Qur'an tells the tale this way:

> He [Musa] entered the city at a time when its inhabitants were unaware and found two men fighting there—one from his party and the other from his enemy. The one from his party asked for his support against the other from his enemy. So Musa hit him, dealing him a fatal blow. [Musa] said, "This is part of Satan's handiwork. He truly is an outright and misleading enemy."
>
> [Musa] said, "My Lord, I have wronged myself. Forgive me."
>
> So He [God] forgave him. He is the Ever-Forgiving, the Most Merciful.
>
> [Musa] said, "My Lord, because of Your blessing to me, I will never be a supporter of evildoers."
>
> Morning found him in the city, fearful and on his guard. Then suddenly the man who had sought his help the day before, shouted for help from him again. Musa said to him, "You are clearly a misguided man."
>
> But when he was about to grab the man who was their common enemy, he said, "Musa! Do you want to kill me just as you killed a person yesterday? You only want to be a tyrant in the land; you do not want to be a reformer."
>
> A man came running from the furthest part of the city, saying, "Musa, the Council are conspiring to kill you, so leave! I am someone who brings you good advice." So he left there fearful and on his guard, saying, "My Lord, rescue me from the people of the wrong-doers!"[24]

Unlike the Torah's account, in the Qur'an it's unclear whether the Egyptian man that Moses struck dead had been doing anything wrong. The Qur'an emphasizes that Moses fatally struck the Egyptian on the basis of prejudice. Moses instantly assumed that his fellow Hebrew was in the right and fought on his behalf solely on the basis of tribal affinity and the presumption that because the Egyptians were the collective oppressors of the Hebrews, this particular Egyptian individual must have been wronging this particular Hebrew. Immediately after killing the Egyptian, he realizes his moral error, and attributes it to his succumbing to Satan's influence. He repents. He receives God's forgiveness. Then, when pre-

23. Exod 2:12.

24. Qur'an, Sura 28:15–21. English translation by Abdalhaqq and Bewley, excerpted from Yahya, *The Prophet Musa (AS)*, 22–24.

sented with the opportunity to repeat his mistake the next day, he learns from his error and refuses to assist the Hebrew man who has now gotten into another fight and has again attempted to enlist his aid. For this act of refusal he earns the hostility and insult of the Hebrew, just as the Egyptian high authorities begin to conspire against him as well.

The Qur'an has retold this Torah story in a way that amplifies the moral ambiguity of Moses' violent act, and that emphasizes his humility and the redemption he achieves from his willingness to be immediately accountable for moral failings. Moses' strength of character is tested when the Hebrew slave whom he assisted asks him the next day to fight on his behalf again. Moses passes the test by finding the strength to resist this social pressure.

By studying the Qur'an's account of this episode alongside the Torah's, we receive the gift of getting to discuss and learn from two different takes on the same incident. This creates possibilities for learning and dialogue that don't exist if each account is taken alone. For instance, these two texts could be used for Jewish-Muslim interfaith study.

After this pivotal episode, the Qur'an's Moses is a figure who goes on to fight the good fight throughout his life. It's a lonely fight for the truth of the Oneness of God—despite the stubborn resistance of Pharaoh and the weak and fickle devotion of the Hebrews during their forty years of wandering in the wilderness.

Overall, in many ways the Qur'an stresses similar themes to those in the Torah in presenting its "Moses." In the Torah and the Qur'an, we read about the Hebrews as a difficult group—prone to backsliding and repeatedly unappreciative of all that God has done for them. And yet, in some key ways, a different "Moses" emerges from the Qur'an's pages. The sum of the Qur'an's narratives about Moses distances him from the Israelites that he led in a way that the Hebrew Bible does not. Let me offer an example of what I mean.

In the Qur'an, the Hebrews get critiqued for being legal obscurantists who overcomplicate God's instructions, much to Moses' exasperation—a possible polemic against Judaism along the same lines of the caricatures of the Pharisees in the New Testament. In the Sura known as "The Cow," we see this criticism depicted in an episode in which Moses struggles to get the Hebrews to follow a simple direction from God:

And when Musa said to his people, "God commands you to sacrifice a cow," they said, "What! Are you making a mockery of us?"

He said, "I seek refuge with God from being one of the ignorant!"

They said, "Ask your Lord to make it clear to us what it should be like."

He said, "He says it should be a cow, not old or virgin, but somewhere between the two. So do as you have been told."

They said, "Ask your Lord to make it clear to us what color it should be."

He said, "He says it should be yellow, a rich yellow, a pleasure to all who look."

They said, "Ask your Lord to make it clear to us what it should be like. Cows are all much the same to us. Then, if God wills, we will be guided."

He said, "He says it should be a cow not trained to plough or irrigate the fields—completely sound, without a blemish on it."

They said, "Now you have brought the truth."

So they sacrificed it—but they almost did not do it.[25]

Harun Yahya, a Turkish Islamic scholar, has the following to say about this incident:

> As related in the above account [of what happened when Musa related God's instruction that the Hebrews sacrifice a cow], the tribe of Musa constantly raised objections against the commands of God. Only when the command became almost non-practicable, due to the petty details they begged for, they relented. In fact, the command was quite plain: sacrifice a cow. A scrutinizing look into Judaism today will reveal this same stubborn rationale among the Jews. The Talmud, the body of traditional Jewish teaching, includes perplexing details pertaining to daily life and prayers. For instance, from milking an animal, to the use of burning incense, one will find countless details seemingly irrelevant to religion. In Judaism, a person's meticulousness in observance of these details, in his daily life and prayers, is thought to be determinant of his piety. The true essence of piety, on the other hand, that is, faith in God and the day of Judgment, is wholly neglected. As such, Judaism has been changed into a body of rituals with no relevance

25. Qur'an, Sura 2:67–71. English translation by Abdalhaqq and Bewley, excerpted from Yahya, *The Prophet Musa (AS)*, 22–24, 91.

to the fundamentals of faith, such as remembrance of God, mercy of God, and love for Him.[26]

Clearly, this commentary advocates a contemporary anti-Jewish polemic in its teaching about the moral and spiritual failings of the Jews as depicted in the Qur'an's account of the Israelites and the cow. I'm not suggesting that this writer's interpretation speaks for Islam in general; however, his comments do reflect a basic attitude towards Jews that I sense, as a Jew reading the Qur'an in translation, from the Qur'an's treatment of Moses.

Like the Qur'an, the Torah certainly presents Moses as having struggled intensely with the Israelites who escaped slavery, and the Torah is unsparing in depicting the faults of the Israelites. But the Moses of the Torah repeatedly intercedes on behalf of this errant people with the passion of a loving parent, reminding God of the merit of their ancestors, Abraham, Isaac, and Jacob, and of the promises God has made to them regarding their offspring. The Torah emphasizes the covenantal relationship between God and the Israelites, and regards Moses' relationship with God as part of that collective Israelite covenant. The Torah's Moses is certainly exhausted by the Israelites' repeated transgressions during those forty years of wandering in the wilderness, and at one point he even has the biblical equivalent of an *I-can't-stand-these-people-anymore-just-shoot-me-now* moment.[27] And yet, when one reads the Torah, one never gets the sense that Moses is a man whose fate is categorically separated from his people's.

Reading the Qur'anic verses about Moses, I get precisely the feeling that the Qur'an's intent is to underscore the *difference* between Moses, whom God has kept close in heaven as a prophet, and the Jews, whom God has generally found to be troublesome because of their stubborn tendencies towards egregious wrongdoing. To some degree, when it comes to Moses, the Qur'an seems to want to separate the shepherd from his flock.

In the end, I think it comes down to this: the Torah is intensely critical of the Israelites but ultimately sees them in a hopeful, positive light. The Qur'an, on the other hand, is also highly critical of the Israelites, but it sees them as a failed people who botched the privilege of having received prophets and revelations from God, so that God had to offer subsequent

26. Yahya, *The Prophet Musa (AS)*, 91.
27. Num 11:15.

revelations in order to guide humankind (the final and most perfect of these revelations being the Qur'an, of course). In terms of how this key difference emerges through the "Moseses" of each text, both the Torah and the Qur'an vividly depict Moses' frustrations with the Israelites' repeated sins. But the failings of the Israelites described in the Torah form part of a Jewish tradition of moral self-criticism through learning from the failures of one's ancestors, whereas the Qur'an's treatment of the Israelites' failures forms part of an Islamic tradition that criticizes an older religion whose covenant with God has become tainted and is eventually surpassed by God's covenant with Muslims as transmitted through the prophet Muhammad and the Qur'an.

By calling attention to ways that both Christianity and Islam came to portray Moses so that he eventually became a part of both religions' critiques of Judaism, I don't mean to suggest that Islam and Christianity are more negative towards other religions than Judaism is. All three of the Abrahamic religions include the discrediting of other religious traditions in their sacred texts. In the case of Judaism, the Torah predates Christianity and Islam, so while the Torah doesn't discredit those religions, it does go to great lengths to discredit the various polytheistic religions that existed alongside ancient Israel. Chronology, not tolerant enlightenment, is the reason why there are no anti-Christian or anti-Muslim polemics in the Torah.

The Torah asserts an exclusive covenantal relationship between the One God and Israel, a claim that ironically later became an element of anti-Jewish polemics in Christianity and Islam. Each in its own way, Christianity and, later, Islam, went on to claim the mantle of chosenness that the Israelites had assumed for themselves. Christianity and Islam both came to argue that *their* new revelations were continuous with, yet superior to, the Israelite revelation, and that theirs was the final and correct revelation. Once this happened, Jews began to generate their own anti-Christian and anti-Islamic polemical sacred writings as well, and the three-way argument over who is God's favorite has never stopped since. Unfortunately, the relationship between the three faiths has often degenerated into what one of my rabbincal school professors once called a "spiritual pissing contest." "My sacred book is the *real* and only completely accurate one, and *yours* isn't." "No *mine* is." "No, *mine!*" In the midst of this spiritual zero-sum game, "Moses" has been shaped by each of these traditions to support its own theological claims vis-à-vis the other two.

In the final analysis, we see that the Qur'an's "Moses" is a composite figure just as is the Torah's, the New Testament's, and the early rabbis' and medieval Jewish philosophers' respective "Moseses." "Moses" became a figure upon whom the religious leaders of each of the three Abrahamic faiths added their own layerings. The rabbinic tradition remade him into a rabbi par excellence, the recipient of not one but two Torahs at Mount Sinai. Christian tradition made him into the great "Old Testament" Lawgiver, the towering figure of the pre-Christian era in the spiritual life of God. By appearing with Jesus and then gracefully fading into the background, Christianity also presents Moses as a Jew who affirms Christianity's claims about Jesus. Muslim tradition made Moses into a prophet who is exquisitely submissive to God's will despite all manner of tests. Musa is also a faithful servant of God who is meant to be seen quite separately from the rest of his people, who are primarily known for having failed to preserve and follow God's revelations to them.

***

In more recent historical times, the figure of Moses has continued to inspire and to invite new layers of mythologizing. African-Americans and abolitionists drew courage from the biblical accounts of Moses facing down Pharaoh and leading the Hebrew slaves triumphantly to freedom. John Brown, the anti-slavery militant who organized and led a guerrilla raid on a US Armory in 1859, was nicknamed the "Moses" of the abolitionist movement.[28] Harriet Tubman was called "Grandma Moses" after leading countless slaves to freedom along the secret paths of the Underground Railroad. A lecturer in black theology at the University of Birmingham, Dr. Robert Beckford, writes the following on the tremendous importance of Moses' life in black communities worldwide:

> The Exodus story is of fundamental importance to black people, because within it we find a group of people who are enslaved and suffering from both economic and political bondage as well as, at times, genocide and infanticide. They call upon God to help, and what God does is respond by liberating them, crushing their

28. Sylvester, "The African-American: From Slavery to Freedom."

oppressors and leading them into freedom. So the Exodus story has functioned as a paradigm for black people throughout slavery. Also in the contemporary world where the black people have found themselves in bondage, they've called upon God to free them as God freed the Israelites in the Exodus account.[29]

The figure of Moses also resonates in the founding stories of the Mormon Church. Leonard J. Arrington's 1985 biography of Brigham Young is called *Brigham Young: American Moses*. Finally, the contemporary, Latin American–born Liberation Theology movement looks to Moses for inspiration. Professor Christopher Rowland of Queen's College, Oxford, writes, "Moses is seen as the leader of the Liberation movement. He is brought up in the court of King Pharaoh and changes from being on the side of the Egyptian king to siding with the poor slaves. That's one of the most important paradigms for Liberation Theology: the idea of opting for the poor."[30]

It's not surprising that Moses continues to be a compelling figure to various religious, activist, and ethnic groups. He is a great mythic iconoclast and advocate for the downtrodden in a world that never has stopped generating different forms of social oppression, idolatry, and falsehood. He represents the possibility of radical transformation and the triumph of justice in human affairs. He is both the successful leader of a rebellion and the organizer and founder of a new order. He inspires hope and has the capacity to give people living under oppressive conditions the sense that God has not forgotten them, that someday things will be made right in *this* world, if not for them then for their descendants. He confronts the ultimate in earthly political power in his face-offs with Pharaoh, and he encounters the Ultimate Power of the universe in his face-to-face conversations with the Almighty. Anyone who ever summoned the nerve to speak truth to power might think of Moses. Anyone who ever felt unjustly persecuted, or who had to run for her life, or who was misunderstood by his own community might find a friend in Moses.

"Moses" is a composite figure, a collage of stories and agendas, ideas and ideals, and he is a different composite figure depending upon what

29. Beckford, "Moses." Online: http://www.bbc.co.uk/religion/religions/judaism/history/moses_1.shtml#h5.

30. Rowland, "Moses," Online: http://www.bbc.co.uk/religion/religions/judaism/history/moses_1.shtml#h5.

context we find him in. The rabbis' *moshe rabbeynu* ("Moses our rabbi") is a different composite figure than the Qur'an's Musa. Both of these are different still from the "Moses" of African-American churches. As we learned from Robert Alter in chapter 6, composite artistry is a kind of storytelling in its own right, with its own aesthetic and its own conventions. Alter likened the composite artistry used by the redactors of the Torah to a post-Cubist painting, of the sort that presents us with a front view and a side view of a person's face situated together in a way that is jarring, yet fascinating, for us to look at.[31] "Moses" in the Torah is the figure that the redactors gave us by skillfully weaving together multiple source materials about the man and adding some flourishes of their own.

With this chapter, I am making the case that all the generations that have worked with "Moses" in a serious way since the creation of the Torah have taken the Torah's composite "Moses" and added more to it, in some cases painting over elements found in Torah with new colors, and in other cases simply adding more to the existing picture.

So what can we learn today from studying "Moses"? Again, I come back to Alter. When we enter the realm of myth, we are trying to express things that in some ways are "essentially contradictory, essentially resistant to consistent linear formulation."[32] One way societies do that is through Alter's "composite artistry."[33] To understand what we're reading when we read mythic texts formed through composite artistry, we have to throw out the rules that modern Western historical storytelling calls for, such as airtight logical consistency, an absence of internal contradictions, and documented sources that prove who said or wrote this or that. Composite artistry has led many different communities that have fashioned a "Moses" to take a set of mythic materials that they've inherited and rework them—possibly snipping off some bits, covering over certain parts with new layers, adding new material to the entire package, or even adjusting parts of the central story itself.

We learn from "Moses" that certain mythic figures are there for us to interact with as archetypes available for ongoing mythical modification. Recognizing this fact about human beings and our methods of working with the mythic helps us understand ourselves a little bit better. We can

31. Alter, *The Art of Biblical Narrative*, 146.
32. Ibid., 145.
33. Ibid. "Composite Artistry" is the title of chapter 7.

also discern that, whoever the historical Moses may have been, there are certain aspects of his story that make him an enduring and compelling figure for ongoing mythical composite artistry.

Some of those elements include: his courage to speak truth to power; his long journey towards a goal he never reached; his unusual status as an insider-outsider in both an oppressed and a ruling-class community; his growing up in the lap of luxury but siding with the poor and abused nonetheless; his intimate and deeply personal relationship with God; his years of solitude (as a shepherd in Midian); his speech disability and consequent fear of speaking in public; his success as the leader of a slave rebellion; his success as the organizer of a new nation under law; his mistakes, especially involving anger, which played a role in his killing of the Egyptian and, in the Torah account, in his being disqualified from entering the Promised Land. Of all these, I believe one of the reasons "Moses" is such a beloved figure is because of his flaws. He has clay feet, like us, and this gives us hope somehow, hope that we too can be great, perhaps, or hope that such greatness is there within us all even despite our flaws.

By attempting to determine which story elements and character traits are the ones that have attracted so many different kinds of people to the figure of Moses, we begin to uncover some insights about what human beings most admire, what moves us the most. When we give up on insisting that any one religion's or sect's version of "Moses" is the unquestionable truth, we expand into the study of the richly layered and ever evolving figure of "Moses," who is made up partly from our ancestors' ideas and stories throughout the centuries, partly from stories that came from witnesses to the historical Moses, and partly from us.

Epilogue

Moses Reminds Us that It's Never Too Late

MY WIFE WORKS IN the unusual field of prison higher education. Once she told me a story about an inmate—I'll call him "Tony"—whom she met during one of the groups she was facilitating. Tony was known throughout the prison for his warm smile and genuinely friendly disposition. She found Tony to be authentically positive in his outlook, and she was struck by the palpable attractiveness of his demeanor. Reflecting on the sweetness of his smile, she said to me, "I just found myself asking, 'How the hell did this guy end up doing a life sentence for murder?'"

"I don't know," I said. "Maybe it was a one-time thing, a terrible moment in his youth, an impulsive act that really doesn't correspond to his essence as a person. Or maybe over the years he changed."

My thoughts then turned to Moses. Moses, who murdered the Egyptian. It was an impulsive act of outrage, possibly done at the peak of his youth as an adult male, the time in his life when he was probably most likely to do such a thing.[1]

In my experience in the Jewish community, we tend to pause for a somber moment when we remember that Moses committed murder, but then this piece of his history recedes to the background of the drama of his life story. By the time we're reading about Moses receiving the laws at

1. Rabbinic tradition teaches that Moses was forty years old at the time of this incident, but the Bible itself does not state his age. I am offering my own interpretation in this case, based on the way I read the biblical text on its own.

129

Mount Sinai, we've pretty much forgotten all about that one violent moment. But maybe we misread the Torah's presentation of Moses in minimizing this part of his life. I'd be willing to bet that Moses never forgot that murder. I'll bet that images of it stayed with him all his life. The moment he launched himself at the Egyptian in fury, the look on the man's face as he struck him, the sound of the blow, the cracking of the man's skull, the blood, the frozen features of the man's face in death: the unforgettable horror of it. The confusion he felt in the immediate aftermath. That first restless, paranoid, sleepless night. Murdering someone changes a person's life forever. Even soldiers in modern warfare who kill from a great distance using hi-tech weaponry suffer PTSD afterward. Moses killed someone up close, with a rock or with his bare hands. Whether he meant the blow to be fatal or not, it was. He saw the life leave the man's body. He saw the man's face. He even buried the body. And we don't really talk about all of this in connection with him. We pause for a moment at the part of the Torah that describes this incident, and then we leave it, buried somewhere in the sands of Egypt.

But I don't think the Torah means for us to forget or minimize Moses' act of murder. The murder takes place at a crucial moment in his growth and identity formation. He has lived in the Egyptian court, knowing for some time about his Hebrew origins as well. The text states that he went out to see the lot of his fellow Hebrews, working at brick and mortar. "Who am I?" he seems to be asking himself. "Who are my brothers? The Egyptians I live with and am accepted among, or these miserable slaves? I need to see more in order to know."

Quickly the veil of innocence is torn from him. He sees an Egyptian overseer brutalizing a Hebrew slave. *Who is my brother?* must have immediately become an overloaded question. Suddenly, embracing the Hebrew as the brother he was duty bound to defend, he murdered his Egyptian brother, and then buried his body in the sand.

Much like Cain before him. This episode, I would argue, calls our attention back to Genesis' account of the first murder in human history. Even though Cain's motive was jealousy and Moses' motive was moral outrage and concern for a victim of violence, I think the Torah intends for us to read these as parallel episodes, in dialogue with each other and commenting on each other.

Note that in the act of killing, Cain strikes a blow to his brother, Abel, when no one else is around to see, just as Moses checks to make sure no one is looking, and then strikes down the Egyptian. Both of these murders are done up close, committed in wrath, by a direct blow from the hand of the perpetrator. Both Moses and Cain hope to conceal the act, unsuccessfully. Like Moses, the evidence of Cain's murder lies in the ground: "And [God] said, 'What have you done? The voice of your brother's blood is crying out to me from the ground?'"[2] Both men have to flee their homelands following their respective murders, never to be the same again.

It's my belief that in the Torah's telling of the story of Moses killing the Egyptian, at the moment in which we read that the Egyptian is dead, we are meant to seize up in anxious suspense because we remember the terrible judgment that Cain was dealt. We know that Cain was marked by his act forever, that he would never be able to rid himself of the horror of his act, that he was condemned to wander. He became an exiled man, a journeyman without a home. So we apprehensively wonder, *what will happen to Moses now?*

At first, it looks like Moses' fate may play out similarly to Cain's. He is forced to flee his homeland and take refuge in no-man's-land. He becomes a wanderer in the forbidding wilderness of the Sinai desert. But then Moses' story differs from Cain's. In the place of his banishment, Moses finds an opportunity to begin a long, slow process of rebuilding the healthiness of his shattered soul.

At Jethro's encampment, Moses begins to serve a long sentence, not so unlike my wife's acquaintance in the prison, Tony. Moses' physical world becomes very small, much like a prison inmate's. He lives within Jethro's wilderness camp, working a daily routine shepherding sheep among craggy, dry hills, under a punishing sun. Years become decades, and the man grows older, spending all of his youth and middle age within this small, remote place doing monotonous, solitary work.

And then, after all this time has passed, the Torah tells us that Moses had developed the quality of humility to unparalleled human heights. Why humility? Perhaps the time he had served had made him humble. Like a modern-day prison inmate serving a long sentence, Moses spent the best years of his life removed from civilization and confined by deadening routine.

2. Gen 4:10—translation mine.

It's after these things have passed in his life that he, one day, has the experience that causes him to realize that the light within him has not been completely extinguished by his act of murder. It happens when he takes a second look at a little plant in the hills—a small heap of thistles and twigs—that has caught fire in the pulverizing desert sun. When Moses stops to look closely at the bush, what he is struck by is not the fire but that the body of the withered plant is not destroyed by this fire. The burning bush is a mirror, and looking in it Moses sees that there is still life, and even higher purpose, within him. The bush symbolizes the divine light within him, concealed from his own view all these years by his shame and distress, from all those years he served the sentence of Cain. It's then that he hears the Divine voice, calling him to fulfill his potential and find his destiny.

By the time Moses takes the stage as God's representative in liberating the Hebrews, he has become someone radiant and spiritually powerful. He has become the kind of person whom people remember and respect. Like my wife's student, Tony, Moses has become someone about whom one might have asked, "How the hell did someone like this murder someone? I just don't see it."

The story of Moses' murder of the Egyptian is crucial to our understanding of how Moses can be relevant to our contemporary lives. Mythically, his story offers us an archetype of the possibility of redemption after terrible mistakes. What do we learn from this story?

We're offered a description, in the language of myth, of what the road to recovery from big mistakes—big sins, if you prefer that language—looks like. Cain's dreaded fate is not the Bible's final word on what must happen to someone who commits a terrible sin. Remember the Jerusalem-based Bible scholar Judy Klitsner, whose book *Subversive Sequels in the Bible: How Biblical Stories Mine and Undermine Each Other*, makes the argument that the Bible presents repeated or parallel stories for the purpose of reconsidering and reworking its ideas and conclusions about them? I think that's what's going on with the texts we're considering here. With Moses' life story, the Torah mines and undermines Cain's murder of Abel in an amazing way. Not only can there be some kind of redemption after even the worst of sins, but there can even be spiritual and moral greatness. But the road we have to walk to repair, or transcend, the damage we've done to our souls is a long and difficult road. It's a road in which we need to cease doing further harm, and then cultivate humility.

In our lives here and now, many if not most of us live with regrets that we carry as painful aches within. Some of us have struggled with addictions. Some of us are haunted by youthful mistakes that caused great harm. Some of us sabotage ourselves or our families by making midlife mistakes. Some of us are punished for our mistakes by official authorities, some not. One thing's for sure: all of us suffer within, and all of us bear the mark of our actions.

Moses teaches us that we are flawed yet resilient beings filled with potential to transform and reembrace the goodness within. The life force within us draws its light from an unending fount of goodness, and that light does not go out even after we've done very bad things. In order to find ourselves face to face with that light, however, like Moses seeing the burning bush, we need to go through a positive, successful transformational process which is not fast or easy. Moses' story teaches that that process includes getting out of the environment in which the terrible sin was committed, and finding a discipline or practice that cultivates new perspective and humility. The teaching is that hope and new potential are more powerful forces in the universe than violence, cruelty, and sin, but that redirection and patient dedication are necessary for us to be able to rebuild our lives anew. Moses teaches us through his mistakes as well as his heroic accomplishments, and his difficult path to personal redemption offers us instruction and hope.

Moses' episode of murder also teaches that even justifiable killing damages our souls. (After all, one could argue that Moses' act, though impulsive, was at least quasi-justified since his target was brutalizing an innocent victim.) Nevertheless, the story's literary parallels to Cain's murder place the spiritual impact of Moses' actions in the same realm as Cain's. Killing damages the killer's spirit. In American society, we see this reality playing out in the large numbers of US military veterans who have come home from Iraq or Afghanistan with PTSD and other trauma-related difficulties.

From the remove of over three thousand years, Moses remains our teacher—in his imperfection, his struggle, his confusion, as well as in his courage, his commitment, and his leadership. Judaism never treated him as a god, but rather as its flawed, greatest hero. This embrace of Moses' humanity in Jewish tradition began with the Torah's assertion that Moses' burial place is unknown and unknowable, thus denying him a burial shrine where he could potentially become an object of worship. Like the Egyptian whose body he buried anonymously in the sand, Moses' body was also, ironically, hidden away in burial. Even the location of the mountain he ascended in his greatest moment of spiritual grandeur, Mount Sinai, is not known in Jewish tradition. So much of his story is left beyond our reach, in the wilderness of the mythic; and yet, with his broken and magnificent life, Moses speaks to us in our confused, cluttered, and compromised condition, here and now.

Bibliography

Abdalhaqq, Hajj, and Aisha Bewley. *The Noble Qur'an: A New Rendering of its Meaning in English*. Norwich, UK: Bookwork, 1999.

Alter, Robert. *The Art of Biblical Narrative*. New York: Basic Books, 1981.

Armstrong, Karen. *The Battle for God*. New York: Ballantine, 2001.

Auerbach, Elias. *Moses*. Translated and edited by Robert A. Barclay and Israel O. Lehman. Detroit: Wayne State University Press, 1975.

Beckford, Robert. "Moses." No pages. Online: http://www.bbc.co.uk/religion/religions/judaism/history/moses_1.shtml#h5.

Bell, John. "Moses." No pages. Online: http://www.bbc.co.uk/religion/religions/judaism/history/moses_1.shtml#h5.

Borg, Marcus J. *Reading the Bible Again for the First Time: Taking the Bible Seriously but Not Literally*. New York: HarperSanFrancisco, 2001.

Briggs, John, and F. David Peat. *Seven Life Lessons of Chaos: Timeless Wisdom from the Science of Change*. New York: HarperCollins, 1999.

Buber, Martin. *Moses: The Revelation and the Covenant*. New York: Harper Torchbooks, 1958.

———. *The Way of Man: According to the Teaching of Hasidism*. 2nd ed. London: Routledge, 2002.

Carasik, Michael. *The Commentators' Bible—The JPS Miqra'ot Gedolot: Exodus*. Philadelphia: Jewish Publication Society, 2005.

Center for Religious Freedom of Hudson Institute with the Institute for Gulf Affairs. *2008 Update: Saudi Arabia's Curriculum of Intolerance*. Washington, DC: Center for Religious Freedom, 2008. Online: http://www.hudson.org/files/pdf_upload/saudi_textbooks_final.pdf.

Eskenazi, Tamara Cohn, and Andrea L. Weiss. *The Torah: A Women's Commentary*. New York: URJ, 2008.

Fox, Everett. *The Five Books of Moses: The Schocken Bible, Volume 1. A New English Translation with Commentary and Notes*. New York: Schocken, 1995.

Friedman, Richard Elliott. *The Bible with Sources Revealed*. San Francisco: HarperOne, 2005.

Gottwald, Norman K. *The Hebrew Bible: A Socio-Literary Introduction*. Philadelphia: Fortress, 1985.

Greenberg, Moshe. "Moses." In *Encyclopedia Judaica*, 12:378–88. Jerusalem: Keter, 1973.

Bibliography

Haaretz. "West Bank Rabbi: Jews Can Kill Gentiles Who Threaten Israel." November 9, 2009.

Harris, Maurice. "Jews and Fellow Travelers: Appreciating the Gifts of Non-Jewish Partners." *Reconstructionism Today* 12.3 (2005) 1, 4–7.

Hartman, David. *Maimonides: Torah and Philosophic Quest.* Philadelphia: Jewish Publication Society, 1976.

Heschel, Abraham Joshua. *Man Is Not Alone.* Philadelphia: Jewish Publication Society of America, 1951.

Holtz, Barry W. "Parashat Shavu'ot." No pages. Online: http://www.jtsa.edu/Conservative _Judaism/JTS_Torah_Commentary/Shavuot_5769.xml.

Johnson, Alan. "Hamas and Antisemitism." No pages. Online: http://www.guardian. co.uk/commentisfree/2008/may/15/hamasandantisemitism.

Kaplan, Mordecai. *The Future of the American Jew.* Jenkintown, PA: Reconstructionist, 1981.

Keen, Sam. *Hymns to an Unknown God: Awakening the Spirit in Everyday Life.* New York: Bantam, 1994.

Kirsch, Jonathan. *Moses: A Life.* New York: Ballantine, 1998.

Klitsner, Judy. *Subversive Sequels in the Bible: How Biblical Stories Mine and Undermine Each Other.* Philadelphia: Jewish Publication Society, 2009.

Lerner, Michael. *Jewish Renewal: A Path to Healing and Transformation.* New York: Grosset/Putnam, 1994.

Levenson, Jon D. *Sinai and Zion: An Entry into the Jewish Bible.* New York: Harper & Row, 1985.

Levitt, Rabbi Joy, and Rabbi Michael Strassfeld. *A Night of Questions: A Passover Haggadah.* Jenkintown, PA: Reconstructionist, 1999.

Manji, Irshad. *The Trouble with Islam Today.* New York: St. Martin's Griffin, 2003.

Nadborny-Burgeman, Nechama S. G. "Ascent and the Terrorist War from Lebanon: A Kabbalistic View of Israel's War with Hizbullah." No pages. Online: http://www .ascentofsafed.com/cgi-bin/ascent.cgi?Name=war66-nechama.

Navon, Chaim. *Genesis and Jewish Thought.* Translated by David Strauss. Jersey City, NJ: KTAV, 2008.

"Online Quran Project." Translated by M. H. Shakir. No pages. Online: http://www .al-quran.info/?x=y#&&sura=8&aya=1&trans=en-shakir&show=both,quran- uthmani&ver=2.00.

Plaskow, Judith. "Dealing with the Hard Stuff." *Tikkun* 9.5 (1994) 57. Online: http://www .tikkun.org/nextgen/dealing-with-the-hard-stuff.

Rowland, Christopher. "Moses." No pages. Online: http://www.bbc.co.uk/religion/ religions/judaism/history/moses_1.shtml#h5.

Safi, Omid. *Memories of Muhammad: Why the Prophet Matters.* San Francisco: HarperOne, 2009.

Scheinerman, Rabbi Amy. "Change and Second Chances / B'haalotekha—May 23, 2010." No pages. Online: http://taste-of-torah.blogspot.com/2010_05_01_archive.html.

Sheridan, Rabbi Sybil. "Moses." No pages. Online: http://www.bbc.co.uk/religion/ religions/judaism/history/moses_1.shtml#h5.

Signer, Michael. "Visions, Conclusions, and Beginnings." No pages. Online: http://www .bajcvermont.org/torah/5768-vaetchanan.pdf.

Spong, John Shelby. *The Sins of Scripture: Exposing the Bible's Texts of Hate to Reveal the God of Love.* San Francisco: HarperSanFrancisco, 2005.

Stein, Jonathan. "The Divine Kiss." No pages. Online: http://urj.org/learning/torah/archives/deuteronomy/?syspage=article&item_id=17300&printable=1.

Sylvester, Melvyn. "The African-American: From Slavery to Freedom." No pages. Online: http://www.liu.edu/cwis/CWP/library/aaslavry.htm.

Tomek, Vladimir. "Passages Advocating Violence and Genocide in Religious Texts." No pages. Online: http://www.religioustolerance.org/tomek24.htm.

Trembling Before G-d. Directed by Sandi Simcha Dubowsky. Working Films, 2001.

Visotzky, Burton L. *Reading the Book: Making the Bible a Timeless Text.* New York: Schocken, 1996.

———. *The Road to Redemption: Lessons from Exodus on Leadership and Community.* New York: Crown, 1998.

Webb, Val. *Like Catching Water in a Net: Human Attempts to Describe the Divine.* New York: Continuum, 2007.

Weinfeld, Moshe, and S. David Sperling. "Ruth, Book of." No pages. Online: http://www.jewishvirtuallibrary.org/jsource/judaica/ejud_0002_0017_0_17192.html.

Yahya, Harun. *The Prophet Musa (AS): The Life and Struggle of the Prophet Musa (AS) in the Qur'an.* New Dehli: Millad, 2002.

Yanklowitz, Shmuly. "Genocide in the Torah: The Existential Threat of Amalek." No pages. Online: http://www.myjewishlearning.com/beliefs/Issues/War_and_Peace/Combat_and_Conflict/Types_of_War/Genocide.shtml.

Zohar, Danah, and Ian Marshall. *The Quantum Society: Mind, Physics, and a New Social Vision.* New York: Quill/William Morrow, 1994.